THE
PSYCHOLOGICAL WARFARE DIVISION
SUPREME HEADQUARTERS
ALLIED EXPEDITIONARY FORCE

AN ACCOUNT OF ITS OPERATIONS IN THE
WESTERN EUROPEAN CAMPAIGN, 1944–1945

Published by Books Express Publishing
Copyright © Books Express, 2011
ISBN 978-1-78039-125-0

Books Express publications are available from all good retail and online booksellers. For publishing proposals and direct ordering please contact us at: info@books-express.com

INDEX

		Page
Foreword		3
I	Introduction	5
II	Background	9
III	Nature of Psychological Warfare	12
IV	Plans and Directives Section	16
V	Operation of PWD Intelligence	20
VI	Radio	25
VII	Leaflets	31
VIII	Special Operations	40
IX	Allied Information Service	44
X	Publications and Display	49
XI	Press	57
XII	Cinema	59
XIII	Pictorial Section	61
XIV	Strasbourg Episode	62
XV	Displaced Persons	66
XVI	Control of German Information Services	69
XVII	The Newspaper at Aachen	71
XVIII	Communications	73
XIX	Financial and Business Management	77
XX	Supply and Transport	79
XXI	The Problem of Newsprint	80
XXII	Status of Control of German Information Services in the American Zone as of the end of September 1945	83

Appendix "A"	SHAEF Operation Memorandum No. 8 (The PWD Charter)	89
" "B"	Voice of SHAEF-Texts (Beginning with No. 68)	90
" "C"	Military Government Talks (These talks undertook to explain to the German people what lay in store for them under Allied Occupation. They were used on the radio and in leaflets) (Beginning with No. 11)	95
" "D"	Standing Directive for Psychological Warfare Against Members of the German Armed Forces	96
" "E"	Psychological Warfare Operations against German Army Commanders to Induce Surrender (Recommendations to G-3 from PWD relative to Development of technique based on experience to date - November 13, 1944)	104
" "F"	Final Report on Leaflet Operation	107
" "G"	PWD Organization Chart	125
" "H"	Organization Chart of Information Control Division, Headquarters, U. S. Forces European Theater and Information Control Service, U.S. Group Control Council (German)	127

FOREWORD

The account which follows is by no means a definitive history of the Psychological Warfare Division (PWD) SHAEF. It does not presume to relate everything that PWD did. The aim has been to describe the development of the organization, the operations in which it engaged, and to give, where possible, the circumstances in which this development took place.

In general, the activities of PWD appeared to fall into three categories: (a) operations against the enemy in the field and at home, and operations directed toward Occupied peoples, (b) so-called consolidation operations in liberated Allied area, (c) control of German information services.

The work of at least one operating section, Leaflets, was involved solely with (a) above. It had no functions in consolidation or relative to German information services. Others, however, like Radio, covered all three areas of activity.

An attempt has been made to describe the activities of the various operating sections in two parts. Where a section dealt in both combat and consolidation fields, these have been described together. The German control operation, on the other hand, has been described separately. Thus, although the German control experiment with the newspaper in Aachen began long before the surrender of the Wehrmacht, it is described separately from the consolidation press operations in France.

A separate chapter has been allotted to Special Operations, rather than to attempt to detail the activities of the various media sections in each such operation.

The background of the activities of the Allied Information Service—the name under which PWD operated in friendly liberated countries—also is described in a separate chapter, but in a rather general way. More details of the activities of the various media in AIS are given in the special chapters allotted to them. Because of the unique character of the PWD operation and because of the ebb and flow of personnel, certain files concerning minor details are necessarily lacking. However, it is submitted that the broad philosophy underlying the missions and accomplishments of PWD is clearly defined.

I. INTRODUCTION

Psychological Warfare Division, Supreme Headquarters Allied Expeditionary Force, was a special staff division of SHAEF charged with responsibility for the prosecution of psychological warfare in the area of continental Europe controlled by the Supreme Commander. Unlike the other divisions of SHAEF, PWD had both staff-planning and operational functions.

The missions of PWD were:

(a) To wage psychological warfare against the enemy.

(b) To use the various media available to psychological warfare to sustain the morale of the people of friendly nations occupied by the enemy and to cause the people of these countries to acquiesce in the wishes of the Supreme Commander.

(c) To conduct so-called Consolidation Propaganda operations in liberated friendly countries.

(d) To control information services in Allied-occupied Germany.

Propaganda against the enemy fell into two categories:

(a) Combat propaganda, which is tactical propaganda conducted in the forward areas and toward those relatively limited groups of the populations immediately behind the enemy lines.

(b) Strategic propaganda, the function of which is to further long-term strategic aims.

Propaganda also divides into three categories along another line. There are white, black, and gray propaganda.

In its simplest terms, white propaganda is propaganda whose source is clearly indicated.

In black propaganda, an attempt is made to cause the target audiences to believe that the source is something other than it really is.

Gray propaganda falls between the other two. Its source is not indicated one way or another.

PWD was the agency which coordinated psychological warfare operations within the jurisdiction of the Supreme Allied Commander. However, it must be borne in mind that certain civilian agencies of the British and American governments dealt in strategic propaganda, which, because of the range of powerful radio transmitters, entered this theater.

Beyond this, political policy directives under which PWD operated stemmed originally from civilian agencies. The political policies of America and Britain are developed by the State Department and the Foreign Office. The propaganda aspects of these policies were developed on the American side by the Office of War Information and on the British side by the Political Intelligence Department of the Foreign Office (PID) and the Ministry of Information (MOI). Directives governing these propaganda policies reached PWD through military channels, however, and with the approval of the Combined Chiefs of Staff. Thus, although the origins of PWD's directives were civilian in character, the operation of PWD itself was a military one under military command.

It is obvious that this dual nature of PWD implied an unusual intricacy of relationships.

Psychological Warfare Division, SHAEF was the first agency, military or civilian, to coordinate successfully in Western Europe the efforts of the numerous military and civilian agencies which had waged Anglo-American psychological warfare since the beginning of the war.

On the American side there had existed for some years in MIS, G-2, War Department, a small Psychological Warfare Section. In the late summer of 1941, a few months before Pearl Harbor, the Office of the Coordinator of Information (COI) was established in Washington. The COI had within it the elements which later were separated into the Office of Strategic Services (OSS) and the Overseas Branch of the Office of War Information (OWI). The COI initiated official American government short wave broadcasts to enemy and enemy-occupied countries in the Autumn of 1941.

On the British side, PID, MOI and the BBC were directing broadcasts and dropping leaflets on enemy and enemy-occupied countries from the beginning of the war in September, 1939.

In the Autumn of 1942—after the COI was split into OSS and OWI—the London Liaison Section of OWI, and PID, agreed to issue each week a Joint Psychological Warfare Directive to which the various psychological warfare agencies of the two countries would be subject. This was the first major instance of practical cooperation between the psychological warfare agencies in Britain and America. This Joint Directive continued as the political policy directive for PWD until the end of its operations.

The closest lineal ancestor of PWD/SHAEF appeared in November 1942 when, at the orders of General Eisenhower, a Joint military-civilian Anglo-American Psychological Warfare Unit was attached to Allied Force Headquarters after the Allied landings in French North Africa. This agency was known as the Psychological Warfare Branch, AFHQ, and it laid many of the foundations on which PWD/SHAEF later was to build a much larger and more intricate structure. It was in PWB/AFHQ that the early lessons of Anglo-American civilian-military cooperation were learned and where much of the trial-and-error involved in the new field of combat psychological warfare operations was undergone. Certain of the personnel which had had experience in PWB later became a part of PWD. Brigadier General Robert A. McClure, Chief of PWD, had been Chief of the Information and Censorship Section of Allied Force Headquarters, of which PWB was a branch.

Even before the end of the Battle for Tunisia, on April 29, 1943, the first discussions leading to the formation of PWD were being conducted in London. On that date a meeting was held at the War Office to discuss the organization of the Intelligence Directorate at COSSAC and during the course of the meeting reference was made to the need for a separate division for Publicity and Propaganda Warfare activities in order to divorce such responsibilities from Intelligence. Two months later, a plan for the creation of a Directorate of Press and Propaganda (DPP) was submitted to the Joint Intelligence Committee of the War Cabinet and approved by them. This was on June 29, 1943. The next day this plan was approved by the Chiefs of Staff Comittee.

On July 5, Lt. Colonel Thor M. Smith was appointed by ETOUSA as the United States representative on the DPP Planning Staff. During the next three months the DPP plan reached the chart stage and copies were circulated to all concerned in Britain and America. In October the name Press and Propaganda was changed to Publicity and Psychological Warfare.

Late in October the Combined Chiefs of Staff in Washington agreed to the DPP plan in principle but decided to leave the staff organization to the decision of the Supreme Commander when he should be named. The Combined Chiefs of Staff recommended that there be two heads, one British and one American, for the Publicity and Psychological Warfare Division. The British Chiefs of Staff

Committee did not concur and urged reconsideration of the single head principle. On November 11, 1943 the U.S. Chiefs of Staff replied that the decision should be left to the Supreme Allied Commander. On November 13 Brigadier General McClure arrived in London from AFHQ to assume the duties as chief of the Publicity and Psychological Warfare Division.

On February 14, 1944 Brigadier General McClure was appointed Assistant Chief of Staff, G-6, which was the new designation of the P and PW Division. On April 13 announcement was made of the discontinuance of the G-6 Division as a general staff division of SHAEF. In its place two special divisions were announced. One was the Public Relations Division under Brigadier General Thomas J. Davis and the other, the Psychological Warfare Division under Brigadier General McClure. The SHAEF General Orders announcing the foregoing also stated that, where necessary, the Public Relations Division and the Psychological Warfare Division would share communications and censorship facilities.

Although the internal organization of PWD/SHAEF changed materially through the months, PWD's relationship to other Staff Divisions and to the Supreme Allied Commander remained substantially the same from this point onward until the dissolution of SHAEF.

SHAEF was dissolved officially as of 2400 hours 13 July 1945. With the dissolution of SHAEF, the Anglo-American aspect of PWD's operation disappeared. On the British side an organization known as the Information Services Control Branch, Control Commission for Germany, came into being. On the American side, the successor to PWD was designated the Information Control Division, Hqs. U.S. Forces European Theater, and the Information Control Service, U.S. Group Control Council. Brigadier General McClure was Chief of both of these American organizations.

The reader should recognize that despite these changes in designation, and despite the separation as between Britain and America, the activities of the successors to PWD continued separately in much the same paths on July 14 as they had been traversing jointly before midnight on July 13.

However, since this is not a history of psychological warfare and its corollaries in general but of PWD/SHAEF, no more than a glimpse of what lay beyond the date of the dissolution of SHAEF can be given here.

*

Through most of the life of PWD, until the beginning of the German Information Control operation, the Chief of PWD was assisted by four deputies, one representing each of the four civilian agencies which contributed personnel to PWD, namely, OWI, OSS, PID, and MOI. For a period there was a fifth who served as the Chief's deputy on purely military matters.* Some months before the German surrender, the civilian deputy representing OSS was withdrawn for other duties, and later the post of military deputy was abolished.

While the four civilian deputies functioned, the various operating sections were divided among them as their primary responsibilities.

These sections were:
(a) Plans and Directives
(b) Intelligence
(c) Radio
(d) Leaflets
(e) Press
(f) Films
(g) Publications and Display
(h) Special Operations

Civilian and military administration, warehousing-transport-supply, and personnel were placed under the Executive Office.

---
* The deputies were: Mr. C. D. Jackson (OWI); Mr. R. H. S. Grossman (PID); Mr. Dennis Routh (MOI); Mr. Fred Oechsner (OSS); Colonel Harold D. Kehm.

For a time there was also a post known as Chief of Operations whose occupant functioned below the deputies and above the operating sections. This post was abolished early in July 1944.

In AFHQ, PWB (the prototype of PWD/SHAEF) had performed all staff and operational functions in the field of psychological warfare. A history of all psychological warfare activities in AFHQ and a history of PWB/AFHQ could not but be the same paper. This was not literally true of PWD/SHAEF.

SHAEF Operation Memorandum No. 8 dated March 11, 1944, defined the responsibilities for the control, coordination, and operation of psychological warfare within the Allied Expeditionary Force. In paragraph 5B under the title "Combat Propaganda," the memorandum stated that "combat propaganda will be confined within the terms of directives issued by SHAEF to *Army Groups* and, as necessary, to Allied Naval Expeditionary Force and Allied Expeditionary Air Force." Paragraph 5O then stated "In order to execute psychological warfare plans prepared under these directives, Army Groups will raise, administer and operate psychological warfare field operational units capable of carrying out" these activities.

Paragraph 6 of the memorandum, titled „Consolidation Propaganda," stated that consolidation propaganda would normally be carried out by Supreme Headquarters, Allied Expeditionary Force. When desirable and practicable, tasks will be decentralized to Army Groups under special directives." Finally, paragraph 7 of the memorandum re-emphasized that "the successful outcome of psychological warfare demands centralized control and coordination of propaganda themes and aims. Any departure from the principle can only lead to ineffective or disastrous results." Sub-paragraph C under paragraph 7 stated that "Any departure required by Commanders-in-Chief (Commanding Generals), Army Groups, or subordinate commanders from the terms of directives issued to them will be referred to and receive the prior concurrence of Supreme Headquarters."

Thus the conduct of Combat psychological warfare was removed from PWD/SHAEF. On the other hand, Consolidation Propaganda operations were made the specific responsibility of SHAEF. Finally PWD/SHAEF's policy control of Army Group Psychological Warfare through directives was established.

Within the context of Operation Memorandum No. 8, PWD/SHAEF's general functions were:

(a) Staff planning.
(b) Issuance of policy directives to Army Groups.
(c) Supply of certain personnel and equipment to Army Group combat teams.
(d) Supervision of training of personnel for Army Group teams.
(e) Production and dissemination of leaflets by strategic aircraft.
(f) Certain strategic radio.
(g) Consolidation propaganda in friendly liberated countries.

[This was done by a separate organization stemming from PWD which was known as Allied Information Service (AIS).]

(h) Operation of captured fixed radio transmitters on the continent.
(i) Liaison assistance in certain circumstances to G-1 and G-5.
(j) Control of information services in Germany.

This paper will attempt to describe in some detail all of the foregoing functions.

II. BACKGROUND

In order to explain the exact nature of PWD's coordinating function in psychological warfare in the area controlled by the Supreme Commander, it appears necessary to give here a brief description of the psychological warfare activities which were going on in this general area before PWD came into being

The most important single instrument for psychological warfare in this area was the British Broadcasting Corporation. The European Service of the BBC, using many powerful transmitters, represented the official voice of the British government tho the people of Europe, whether enemy, enemy-occupied, or neutral Beyond this, because of the proximity of Britain to the Continent, the BBC Home Service, in its own way, was an instrument for psychological warfare since its signal was audible on the Continent.

The BBC functioned under its own directives which were based on the PID directives, and, later, on the Joint OWI/PID directives referred to in Chapter I of this paper.

In America, certain short wave transmitters controlled by the OWI beamed programs in many languages to the same audiences as those reached by BBC. As time went on, an increasing number of OWI "Voice of America" programs were relayed by BBC under the general title "America Calling Europe."

Before D-Day (June 6, 1944) OWI inaugurated broadcasting over transmitters erected in Britain which were linked under the name of the American Broadcasting Station in Europe (ABSIE).

These transmitters—BBC and ABSIE—were managed and operated by the civilian agencies. They continued to be managed and operated by the civilian agencies. Their programs were heard not only within the area controlled by the Supreme Commander, but far beyond those limits as well. However, they formed one of the most important of the media available to PWD. Thus, when shortly before D-Day PWD inaugurated continuing broadcasts of instructions known as "The Voice of SHAEF," BBC and ABSIE were the outlets. Special directives from the Supreme Commander were channeled through PWD for BBC and ABSIE.

In the field of leaflets, as in radio, large scale operations had been conducted by OWI and PID before PWD came on the scene. On the British side, PID had been engaging in leaflet operations since the beginning of the war, using the Royal Air Force as its dissemination medium. OWI had been conducting leaflet operations since the summer of 1942. In the beginning, the RAF was used by OWI in the absence of American aircraft. As time went on, OWI's leaflet operation expanded until a special squadron of B-17s of the Eighth U.S. Air Force was assigned exclusively to this work.

It was against this background of already existing activities that PWD took up the task of coordinating Anglo-American psychological warfare on a military rather than a civilian basis under the specific directives of the Supreme Allied Commander.

In the beginning, PWD was largely without personnel or equipment. It was an idea rather than an operation. In order to pass from the idea stage to the operational stage it was required that the four civilian agencies detail personnel and equipment to PWD. Like the other Divisions of SHAEF, PWD was to utilize British and American personnel interchangeably. Beyond this, and unlike the other Divisions of SHAEF, PWD was to utilize civilian personnel from the four civilian agencies in both planning and operational functions. It must be borne in mind that because of the nature of psychological warfare, and in view of the background of the civilian agencies, civilians at first formed the largest group of trained operational personnel available to PWD.

Despite the experience gained in PWB/AFHQ, the agencies in London did not at first comprehend the relationship that was to exist between them and PWD/SHAEF in the western European military operation. This relationship was, in point of fact, quite simple: all psychological warfare activities against the enemy, and all consolidation propaganda activities conducted in liberated countries were to be conducted or controlled by PWD/SHAEF as the representative of the Supreme Commander. PWD was to be, in effect, the umbrella under which everyone, military and civilian, engaged in psychological warfare activities would function. The civilian agencies were to assign personnel to PWD, and so long as such individuals were on assignment to PWD, they were under the immediate direction of the Chief of PWD and not under the direction of the chiefs of the several agencies. Instructions and directives governing the activities of these individuals did not reach them directly from their original agencies, but through military channels and the office of the Chief of PWD.

It was envisaged that, when military exigencies no longer demanded, military control of Consolidation Propaganda activities and certain of the civilian personnel would be returned to the civilian agencies, which would then take over, on a national rather than joint basis, and as civilians, the continuing tasks which had been begun under military control by PWD.

Under the terms of Operation Memorandum No. 8, referred to in Chapter I of this paper, Army Groups began the task of assembling psychological warfare teams in the early spring of 1944. Only one Army Group, the 21st, was to be in the field at the beginning of the Normandy operation. At the same time, the Headquarters of a U.S. Army Group was located in London. This Army Group was to become operational when the Third U.S. Army would join the First U.S. Army in France. Then the First Army would be withdrawn from 21st Army Group and a purely American Army Group would operate beside the British 21st. The 12th U.S. Army Group became operational in July 1944, and control of the P.W. Team of First U.S. Army reverted to the Psychological Warfare Branch of 12th Army Group.

On the American side, the basis of personnel for psychological warfare in the field was a purely military unit known as a Mobile Radio Broadcasting Company (MRBC). The first MRBC had been assigned to PWD/AFHQ. As time went on, the 2nd, 3rd, 4th, and 5th MRBCs operated with the American armies in France. Other personnel, both military and civilian, was attached for the purposes of lift, administration, etc. to one or another of the MRBCs. On the British side there was no such unit basis as this and personnel was attached to the Psychological Warfare Branch, 21st Army Group on an individual basis.

In both Army Groups, the Psychological Warfare Branch was part of a combined Publicity and Psychological Warfare Division, similar to that which had existed in SHAEF before April 13, 1944, when Publicity and Psychological Warfare were separated.

Assignment of personnel by the civilian agencies and by the British and American forces to PWD/SHAEF proceeded through the late winter of 1943 and spring of 1944. When the Staff-planning sections were complete, PWD/SHAEF began the additional task of re-assigning personnel to Army Groups. On the American side there was a further re-assignment from the Army Group to First U.S. Army. This personnel later was to be brought back to 12th Army Group when it became operational.

PWD, with the aid of certain already established British and American agencies, undertook the screening and training of personnel to be offered for assignment to Army Groups.

At the same time, specific operational planning was going forward within the sections of PWD/SHAEF. A plan for taking over information services in Europe under "RANKIN" CASE C conditions was presented to the Chief of Staff. Later the PWD plans for "OVERLORD" and other operations were completed.

Liaison was initiated with representatives of the several exiled Allied governments in London. Stockpiling of radio, press and publications material was coordinated among the several contributing agencies by PWD. The News Section experimented with a special radio news file which later was to form the basis of press activities on the Continent.

The Leaflet Section undertook to coordinate the separate British (PID) and American (OWI) leaflet operations, and a joint PID/OWI printing-production directorate was set up in order to make the most effective use of these facilities in the United Kingdom.

As has been noted previously, the "Voice of SHAEF" broadcasts began on BBC and ABSIE before D-Day. These were to continue throughout the life of SHAEF and represented the radio aspect of the relatively simple basic pattern that all PWD activities assumed in the Western European operation. PWD, as the articulation of the Supreme Commander to the people of enemy and enemy-occupied countries, utilized all its available media for the simple purpose of telling the various audiences what the Supreme Commander wished them to do, why they should do it, and what they might expect if they carried out the Supreme Commander's wishes. Thus, although PWD/SHAEF did not by any means perform all psychological warfare operations in Western Europe, its directive control was sufficient to permit it to coordinate the efforts of the agencies and individuals which contributed toward the total psychological warfare impact and to coordinate these efforts along the simple line of the Supreme Commander's specific expressed wishes. PWD/SHAEF was the channel that extended back to the political policy-making agencies in London and Washington and forward to the extreme front lines where Psychological Warfare Teams were in immediate contact with the enemy.

III. NATURE OF PSYCHOLOGICAL WARFARE

Although, as noted earlier, the history of PWD/SHAEF and the history of psychological warfare in Western Europe are not coextensive, an overall understanding of the nature of psychological warfare, its ends and means, appears necessary for a thorough comprehension of the place of PWD/SHAEF in the larger picture.

Psychological warfare as a weapon of war is by no means new. In its simplest terms it stems from earliest times. In the first year or two of this war, German psychological warfare was eminently successful as an integral part of the overall German effort against Poland, Norway, France, Belgium, Holland—against all of Germany's eventual adversaries, in fact, except Britain, United States, and Russia.

However, despite this, and despite the role played by Psychological Warfare in the closing months of the last war, Anglo-American psychological warfare was slow in organizing itself for all-out effort. The principles of psychological warfare were understood, but the organization, personnel, and equipment required to put these principles into operation were not immediately forthcoming.

The aims of psychological warfare are to destroy the fighting morale of our enemy, both at home and at the front, and to sustain the morale of our Allies. In the case of both, the ultimate aim is to build up a background of acceptance of what we say to the point where, when the time arrives, the instructions of the Supreme Commander can be transmitted quickly to the audiences for which they are intended, with some hope that these instructions will be acted upon.

In its simplest terms, modern psychological warfare is a vast operation in the field of publicity. Every possible medium of expression must be mobilized in order to achieve the broadest possible coverage. Thus, not only fixed radio transmitters, such as the BBC and ABSIE, are used, but mobile radio transmitters and public address vans. Leaflets are dropped not only by heavy bombers, but by medium bombers and fighter bombers, and they are fired over the lines by artillery, and carried into enemy positions by patrols and agents. Leaflets are printed in millions of copies on large static presses at such bases as the United Kingdom, and also in smaller quantities on mobile presses for immediate use near the front.

Newspapers are published for liberated areas in order to fulfill the people's need for the information which will dispell rumors and assist the appropriate military authorithies in maintaining order and in quickly returning the areas to a semblance of normality.

Where necessary, wall news bulletin are published with the same aim in view. Posters are provided, giving instructions to the newly liberated people. Publications are distributed, continuing the line begun by the more immediate media such as newspapers and posters.

All of these activities necessarily represent a need for speedy communications between the front and the base of operations. They represent both a source and a need for immediate intelligence concerning the areas under operation.

These are the physical aspects of the task. Largely, these aspects have their counterparts in other branches of the total military effort. But there the similarity ceases. The results of psychological warfare are more ephemeral and difficult to assay. For example, leaflets discharged at the enemy by artillery shell cannot be regarded as so many paper bullets calculated to produce the imme-

Leaflet bombs dropped from a B-17 of the 8th U.S. Air Force tumble on **Merseburg**, Germany. (USSTAF Photo.)

diate effect of persuading enemy soldiers to desert. In the latter days of the war, when the German break-up was proceeding rapidly, thousands of deserters came over bearing leaflets as their safe conduct. But this was merely the end result of psychological warfare efforts directed against the enemy since the campaign began. One leaflet or one broadcast by a public address van across the lines will never, save in exceptional cases, achieve the end of causing a soldier to desert unless he was already nearly of a mind to do it anyway. The essence of successful psychological warfare is consistency and repetition. In the larger picture, however, psychological warfare cannot function in a vacuum. It must be tied closely to military events and without the impressiveness of military successes it cannot itself be successful.

PWD had behind it sufficient trial and error experience to understand this most important aspect of its work. In the early days of the war the British leaflets dropped by the RAF on Germany could not but have been without result, since during that first winter of 1939—40 the German people could not possibly have found any logic in the British propaganda that they give up the war. Poland had been overrun with impressive ease and there was nothing on the horizon to indicate to the Germans that anything but continued success lay ahead.

If psychological warfare is in essence a vast task of publicity, similar in many ways to modern advertising, its basic sales argument is the force of military might. And this, of course, requires hard evidence.

Eventually, PWD wished to express the will of the Supreme Commander to cause German soldiers to surrender before they might otherwise have done so. In order to do this PWD had to prove to the German soldier that the will of the Supreme Commander was supported by overwhelmingly superior arms. But during the early period of the Normandy campaign PWD could not call upon the German soldier to surrender because the point of military superiority had not been proved. This required military events. During that early period, PWD concentrated vast efforts against the German soldiers in the West, but the messages involved were mostly simply news bulletins of the progress of the fighting. They were the beginning of a long pressure which, it was hoped, would eventually result in surrenders of German soldiers who came to be convinced of the military evidence on the Allied side.

In the early days of the campaign PWD restricted itself primarily to bringing news to the German soldiers in order to establish an eventual belief in the authenticity of what PWD said. This acceptance could come only when the German soldier had had an opportunity to compare what PWD told him with events as he knew them and against the background of what his own leaders told him. As time went on, and the Allied cause improved and the German retrogressed, the speed with which German soldier after German soldier accepted the Allied version of events increased in geometric progression. This very circumstance is an indication of the extreme importance of complete integration of psychological warfare activities into the planning and operations of a military campaign. Without any knowledge of military plans and lacking a thorough appreciation of the day by day changes in the pressures at the front, psychological warfare would have been a haphazard and almost useless addition to the intricacies of modern large scale warfare.

Since the technique of waging a campaign of psychological warfare depends upon the slow building of acceptance by the audience, it follows that truth is the most important ingredient in psychological warfare. Such truth, to be sure, can, and sometimes must, be selective, for often the truth is not credible to the enemy However, selective or not, use by overt propaganda of falsehoods which can be proved false by the enemy is the same as killing the goose that might eventually lay golden eggs.

While the long process of building up toward acceptance by the enemy went on, psychological warfare had available an immediate and more amenable audience. This audience was composed of the people of enemy-occupied countries. From D-Day onwards PWD addressed, by leaflet and radio, the people of France, Belgium, and the Netherlands, transmitting to them the instructions of the Supreme Commander. In the beginning, these instructions were to sit tight and to await further instructions. This was of extreme importance. Had these people acted prematurely, they would have risked their lives needlessly and would have been lost to the Allies when they were really needed to act as saboteurs, etc. Thus, from the beginning, there was work for PWD to do relative to both of its audiences, namely, friends and foes. The audience of friends presented a relatively easy problem. The audience across the line was more difficult. To the German soldier it had to be proved that his defeat was inevitable; to the German civilian, the same point had to be proved in a different way and in different terms.

As large areas were liberated, PWD used various of its media to guide a bewildered populace and to assist the several national governments to reassume their own information functions after four years of occupation.

Finally, with the defeat of Germany, PWD assumed its ultimate task, that of assisting the military occupying authorities in controlling German thought and expression as the first step toward eventual re-education of the nation. The chapters that follow will attempt to describe in detail the means whereby all of these missions were accomplished.

Description of PWD operations will be divided as between operations prior to the formal occupation of Germany, and operations after that date, the latter concerning control of German information services.

IV. PLANS AND DIRECTIVES SECTION

Troughout the greater part of PWD activity up to the surrender of the German Army Plans & Directives' sub-sections were linked under a single civilian deputy. As is obvious, the work of these two sub-sections was inextricably linked. When overall plans were made for particular operations, directives implementing them were a corollary.

As was noted earlier, the first plan for psychological warfare operations prepared by PWD was written early in 1944, at a time when the organizational structure of PWD was simply a skeleton; and a very slender one at that. This plan presumed to cover PWD operations in the event of a sudden German collapse under conditions known by the code phrase RANKIN—Case C. Much of the work in preparing this plan was done by individuals from OWI and PID who later were to play greater or lesser parts in PWD. The overall plan was prepared in a very few days in response to an urgent demand from the **Chief of Staff, SHAEF**, and, in retrospect, it must be stated that much of the plan as originally put down would have proved inoperable in fact. As time went on, the original RANKIN—Case C Plan was revised in the light of increased knowledge of the problems and conditions.

In the weeks following the preparation of the original **RANKIN—CASE C Plan**, PWD laid its plans for psychological warfare operations involved in the projected invasion of Northwestern France. Operation Memorandum No. 8 was approved by the Chief of Staff and directives covering formation of psychological warfare teams with Army Groups were passed down. Meanwhile, the first important continuing directive for propaganda against the enemy was issued. This covered, in general terms, the subject of propaganda against the German armed forces. A copy of this forms an appendix to this paper. This was available for study before D-Day by PWD/SHAEF headquarters and by members of the combat propaganda teams, which were being assembled in various places outside London.

It will have been noted that under terms of Operation Memorandum No. 8, directive control of psychological warfare operations in Western Europe, whether by SHAEF or by Army Groups, was a primary responsibility of PWD/SHAEF. Some discussion of the background of such control may be pertinent here.

Like so many aspects of PWD/SHAEF and of psychological warfare combat teams in Western Europe, the collateral ancestor of the PWD/SHAEF policy control problem is to be found in PWB/AFHQ. Because it was so completely without precedent, PWB/AFHQ in its early days in the autumn and winter of 1942 appeared to fall between two shools in the matter of policy control. On the one hand, its essentially military character was not immediately understood nor recognized. On the other, the original authority of the various civilian agencies of the Anglo-American governments to formulate political and propaganda policy was not clearly defined within the military organization of the new Anglo-American military theater in the Western Mediterranean. As time passed, however, and the functions of PWB/AFHQ came to be understood by the civilian agencies in Britain and America and by the other echelons of the AFHQ military command, the basis for PWB interpretation of civilian political and propaganda policies in terms of immediate military exigencies was established. This basis did not change, essentially, in PWD/SHAEF.

U.S. artillerymen examine PWD Safe Conduct leaflets preparatory to firing them into enemy lines near Reipertsweiler, Northern Alsace. (U.S. Signal Corps Photo.)

It was simply this:

The basic long-term political policies of the two governments were laid down by the State Department and the Foreign Office. The propaganda policies based on these political policies were developed by the United States Office of War Information and the Political Intelligence Department of the Foreign Office. The Joint Weekly Directive prepared by OWI and PID was the final word. However, it was recognized that there must be a transition from basic civilian political policy to the more immediate needs of the military command in a specific theater. Thus, the Joint OWI/PID Directive came to PWD with the understood approval of the Combined Chiefs of Staff, and it reflected local conditions not immediately available to the home office.

During the early months of PWB/AFHQ faulty communications had inhibited rapid dispatch of the directives from London and Washington to Algiers. As long as this situation persisted, PWB officers were forced to play by ear. Most of these officers had had little or no experience with OWI-PID propaganda policy, and in consequence, there was much straying from the official line. In view of this, it is not surprising that when swift communications became available, the civilian policy-making agencies insisted that the pendulum swing the other way, with the result that despite possible local military exigencies, PWB was ordered to hew strictly to the letter of the official line. Ultimate balance between these two extremes was achieved during the period preceding the abdication of Mussolini and the Italian surrender.

Day by day and hour by hour there were local military and political developments of great importance which could not be known immediately to the civilian policy-making agencies in America and Britain. These developments necessarily had great bearing on PWB's propaganda policy. It soon became manifest that PWB officers were the best qualified to determine propaganda policy in these rapidly changing circumstances.

Thus, pressure of events placed PWB in the position of recommending policy to London and Washington and these recommendations usually were included in the next Joint Directive. Meanwhile PWB was permitted, because of its knowledgeable position, to follow its own suggestions without awaiting formal approval from London and Washington.

This gradual arrival at flexible policy control was reflected in the policy control aspects of PWD/SHAEF. Fortunately, communications between London and the Army Groups, and later, between Paris and Army Groups, always were more efficient than communications between London and the Mediterranean front (via Algiers) had been. In general, policy directives passed smoothly from SHAEF and the lower echelons to front line operating units. Upon occasions, to be sure, during periods of rapid movement, there was an unavoidable time lag, but this was merely the same problem that faced all military units in the field. Sometimes, for instance, details of instructions contained in a radio Voice of SHAEF were not received by psychological warfare combat teams, and the first knowledge that these teams had concerning the Supreme Commander's instructions to various groups of enemy or occupied peoples came to them from the radio. It was difficult under such circumstances to coordinate the strategic psychological warfare operations with immediate plans of Army G-3.

Generally speaking, the texts of the Voice of SHAEF, taken together, represented the regular operational policy contributions of PWD/SHAEF to the continuing OWI-PID policy directives.

The Directives Section provided, in addition, daily guidance notes for Army and Army Group teams and for the civilian agencies at Rear. These notes were based on SHAEF G-2 and G-3 briefings, viewed in the light of PWD's special interest.

Beyond this, the Plans & Directives Section prepared certain special papers, based on accumulated evidence bearing on operational policy. One such paper, containing suggestions for phrasing of ultimata to enemy unit commanders, is attached to this paper as an appendix.

V. OPERATION OF PWD INTELLIGENCE

I. Scope

Psychological Warfare intelligence differs from other military intelligence in the sense that it must gather material not only for an appreciation of the situation but also for actual production in the various media.

The operative echelons in PWD intelligence were the psychological warfare detachments of Armies. These detachments were subject to control by the P an PW Divisions of Army Groups. Since the Armies, under Army Group, were responsible for tactical operations, i. e. short-term propaganda to the adjacent enemy, the primary responsibility for psychological warfare intelligence of a tactical nature rested with Armies. The primary function of the PWD Intelligence Section was to organize and obtain the flow of intelligence required for strategic propaganda.

The PWD Intelligence Section had no chain of command, but operated by suggestion to Army Groups for Armies as to its needs, and from time to time by directives issued by the Chief of PWD on intelligence matters.

II. Source

The primary sources of PWD intelligence were:
a) G-2 material on the enemy's strength, capabilities and intentions.
b) G-3 material on the state of the battle and our potentialities.
c) Interrogation of prisoners of war with special emphasis on psychological warfare matters.
d) Captured enemy documents.
e) Civilian interrogation.
f) Material obtained from other staff sections of each echelon and from the civilian agencies.

III. Organization of Intelligence Missions

The Intelligence Section of PWD/SHAEF, like the other sections, seconded personnel to Army Groups. Psychological Warfare Detachments of Armies were provided with prisoner of war interrogators, document analysts, G-2 liaison officers, and, after entry into Germany, G-5 liaison officers.

French intelligence dealing with the attitudes and state of mind of the French civilian population was an obligation of PWD Intelligence Section from D-Day onwards until December 1944. It functioned through the Allied Information Service, the name under which PWD consolidation work in France was done. A more detailed discussion of the operation of AIS in all sections will be found elsewhere in this paper. AIS operated its own Intelligence Section and the overall directives concerning the types of intelligence required were given by the Intelligence Section of PWD. Reports from the field were evaluated and circulated by this section.

With respect to Belgium and Dutch intelligence, the primary pschological warfare responsibilities devolved upon psychological warfare representatives in the SHAEF Missions to Belgium and the Netherlands. Intelligence officers operated directly under the psychological warfare representative in such missions but special requests were made from time to time by the Intelligence Section and materials required also were obtained for the use of the Missions.

From the end of 1944 PWD Intelligence Section concentrated on German intelligence both with respect to the Wehrmacht and to the German home front.

IV. Organization of PWD Intelligence Section

A. Enemy Documents. The normal flow of captured enemy documents was from regiment or division to G-2 Army and thence to G-2 Documents Section, SHAEF. A PWD liaison officer sat in the G-2 Documents Section, SHAEF for the purpose of obtaining documents of interest to PWD. As this task increased in size, additional personnel was added. The major problem was to work out a system under which G-2 approval could be obtained for release of certain documents for use in propaganda. In the case of documents which PWD wished to use in propaganda, the PWD liaison officer discussed the matter with the appropriate G-2 officer and if the material was releaseable, a buckslip signed by the G-2 officer was attached, giving this permission.

Another problem was to work out an arrangement with the civilian agencies whereby they would be responsible for using the documents under their policy directives concurred in by PWD/SHAEF. PID and OWI agreed to place representatives at PWD Headquarters, to be attached to its staff for the purpose of insuring that documents would be used by the strategic radio. In the later months of war, captured enemy letters, generally taken unopened at a Feldpost, which had always been of interest to PWD, became an object of extreme interest to Radio Luxembourg. Many such letters were obtained by 12th Army Group, but request was made for more and arrangements were effected at SHAEF for the transmission of packets of unopened mail to Radio Luxembourg, which used them on an effective program called "Letters that never arrived."

B. Other relations with G-2. It was recognized at an early stage that proper current guidance required up-to-the-minute information on the state of battle and the enemies' capabilities and intentions. A liaison officer under the direction of the PWD Intelligence Section was placed in contact with G-2, SHAEF principally the Summaries and Order of Battle Sections. It was a continuing difficulty that the overall picture of the battle was obtained separately from G-2 and G-3. G-3 liaison was obtained by the Plans and Directives Section and it was principally on future operations. The Intelligence from G-3 was obtained from the War Room directly by the Intelligence Section with certain additions from Plans and Directives liaison officer.

The Intelligence Section's G-2 liaison officer wrote a daily report, geared as time went on to daily output, including extracts from prisoner of war interrogations, relevant extracts from captured documents, leading enemy military personalities, etc., as well as the state of the battle. This overall report was shown daily to a responsible officer of G-2, SHAEF, who marked the passages which might be used for propaganda and those which were for information only.

The Intelligence Section also held a weekly meeting with the Chief of Operational Intelligence, G-2 to review the position and to discuss various propaganda possibilities based on the enemy's weaknesses and strength. A special G-2 liaison officer was maintained at PWD Rear Echelon in London, who obtained daily briefings from ETOUSA* and the War Office. This was primarily for the benefit of the civilian agencies, since the Main PWD information frequently arrived too late for immediate use.

C. Interrogation of Prisoners of War. As has been shown, intelligence personnel operated at Army Group level and it was understood early that the highest priority on prisoner of war interrogations at Army level must be given to items of a tactical nature. A primary responsibility of PW Army Detachments was to prepare tactical leaflets for immediate use against the enemy. Thus, while certain items of general intelligence would normally be covered, an objective picture of the morale and attitudes of the Wehrmacht could not be obtained entirely from such tactical minded interrogations. Soon after D-Day, therefore, a special team of interrogators, operating directly under the Intelligence Section of PWD, was created. This team conducted objective interrogations of non-selected prisoners for purposes of studying the morale of the enemy and to determine trends in morale. An arrangement was made with the Provost Marshal, ETOUSA for camp facilities at Bourton-On-The-Hill, England where a team taken from the 4th MRBC was installed. This team was sent to France and functioned successfully at various prisoner of war camps in there. It gathered a large flow of material undiluted by any specific propaganda needs of a tactical nature. Standard form questionnaires were prepared with the assistance of the War Office and various trend studies were made.

In addition, there was attached to the Intelligence Section a Survey Sub-section which contucted polls of public opinion among various types of respondents. This section did a certain amount of work in France, mostly on reactions to Allied propaganda in the various media. It did a limited amount of testing of French public opinion on subjects of the day, but was inhibited in this respect by the delicacy of the situation involved in appearing to flaunt French sovereignty. Accordingly, the survey personnel was given the additional task of conducting attitude polls in prisoner of war camps. These results were important in that they provided a quantitative basis for results found qualitatively by individual interrogations.

There were a number of difficulties with the public opinion technique as applied to prisoners. For example, the underlying morale of the Wehrmacht, as evidenced by its behavior in battle, appeared to be a subject not susceptible of measurement by the questionnaire method. Nevertheless, the survey services were useful with respect to determining attitudes of allegiance to Nazi leaders and symbols, fears with respect to Anglo-American potentialities and intentions, and similar matters. It was found, however, that the survey technique required careful editing and appraisal in the light of other media available before conclusions could be drawn.

The technique of drawing the questionnaires was continually being improved by round table discussion. The nuances of German phraseology employed frequently were tested by pre-submission to friendly prisoners of war.

D. Selection of Prisoners for Output. Although this was not strictly speaking a function of the Intelligence Section, the Intelligence Section assumed the responsibilities for reasons of coordination. In any event, the scheme did not work out very well in practice. On the British side, there was some success relative to prisoners located in the United Kingdom due to close relationship between PID and MI-19 of the War Office. On the U.S. side, no adequate liaison was set up sufficiently early to make the American camp authorities an integral part of the selection procedure. The situation became even more difficult when prisoners of war in U.S. custody remained on the continent instead of being trans-shipped to the United Kingdom, for then the initial difficulty was magnified by difficulties of transport. In the later months of the campaign the problem was solved in part by the assignment of an officer to PWD Intelligence Section who travelled from camp to camp and selected prisoners for transport to England. These selected prisoners were prepared for use on the Allied radio by PID and then made available to all interested agencies—British and American. It was the recommendation of the Chief of PWD Intelligence Section that a special section should have been created to deal with this problem as its exclusive province and that jurisdictionally it should have been a part of the Radio Section, which was most vitally concerned with the use of prisoners in output.

E. Relations with G-5. It was a responsibility of PWD/SHAEF to provide G-5 with intelligence concerning civilian morale, etc. Lisaison arrangements between the Intelligence Section PWD/SHAEF and with G-5 were made. Documents were exchanged between PWD and G-5 and it was suggested to interrogators in the field that on matters of reporting affecting G-5 administration or policy, clearances should be sought in the field with responsible officials. PWD worked out a policy with G-5, SHAEF for consultation on all doubtful items of this nature. Such discussions avoided the suggestion of implied criticism, while at the same time reserved to PWD the right to comment on facts found.

In reporting attitudes of German civilians, it was inevitable that there should be criticism of officials appointed by Military Government or even of military government officers. Although this sort of material could be reported strictly as a finding of attitude on public opinion, the invidious reference was, nevertheless, likely to arise. Accordingly, the closest contact with G-5 at all levels was sought to avoid misunderstanding.

In France there was great reliance by G-5 on the intelligence reporting of PWD (in this case it was actually AIS) with respect to the reactions of the civilian population to conditions of life after liberation and to the policies of G-5.

F. The Weekly Paper. Since much of the basis for policy planning as well as for output was to be found in intelligence material, the Intelligence Section of PWD decided that the distribution of raw material *or even material evaluated in hock* was insufficient to meet the overall needs. Consequently, a weekly secret paper was created which carried an analysis of the week dealing with the French situation, the morale of the Wehrmacht, and the German home front. This paper, to be sure, underwent changes based on changing conditions. After a time, the French section was dropped when there was no longer sufficient material available and when the need had passed. The German home front section was divided into the occupied zone, the battle zone, and the home front. Its aim was to be entirely objective and to refrain from accepting the atypical item as significant. In this respect it differed from a propaganda guidance, and the aim was to keep it as far as possible a "pure intelligence" report.

To fill the need for weekly guidance, a composite weekly guidance was put out for the production sections of PWD and for lower echelons. This was written by the Radio Section, after careful discussion and editing in conjunction with Plans and Directives and the Intelligence Section. This paper gave, in coherent form, the material of the week useful for output, while at the same time it sought to retain the minimum objectivity required for white propaganda.

No attempt was made by the Intelligence Section to cover propaganda analysis since this kind of service was adequately provided for by PID and OSS.

G. Evaluation. In London, evaluations originally were done for the Intelligence Section by Duty Rooms jointly staffed by OSS and PID. When PWD Main moved to the continent reliance could no longer be placed on these Duty Rooms for specific evaluation. They were then used for answering questions of a research nature.

H. German Planning. In addition to its other functions the Intelligence Section was responsible for the preparation of "black" and "white" lists of Germans, particulary in the field of radio, press, and theater. It compiled lists of important centers where documents were kept and lists of newspapers, publishers, theaters, cinemas, and It also prepared target studies for seizure of documents by "T" Forces.

I. **Personnel.** Throughout the period of the operations of the Section its staff numbered never more than forty persons, including secretarial and clerical help.

VI. RADIO

I. Scope

PWD/SHAEF radio operations, before the assumption of control of German information services by PWD, fell into the following categories:—
a. Servicing strategic radio.
b. Operation of mobile transmitters in liberated areas.
c. Operation of public address units in liberated areas.
d. Assistance to liberated areas.
e. Operation of captured static transmitter (Radio Luxembourg).

Psychological warfare detachments of Army Groups and Armies operated mobile transmitters against pockets of enemy troops and conducted sound truck operations across the lines to enemy troops. These, however, were not operations of PWD/SHAEF.

II. Servicing Strategic Radio

As was indicated earlier in this paper, the large strategic radio transmitters of the BBC, ABSIE, and Voice of America continued to be operated by the civilian agencies throughout the campaign. However, as D-Day approached, and thence onward, PWD, as the Voice of the Supreme Commander, became more and more involved in the output of these civilian operated transmitters. The "Voice of SHAEF" broadcasts were continuing features on all of them. These began before D-Day, with warnings to the populations of the occupied countries of Western Europe—warnings which gave them the Supreme Commander's instructions concerning their actions under a variety of possible circumstances. PWD Radio Section also planned, coordinated, and assisted in the execution of the large scale D-Day broadcasts which announced the invasion of Normandy to the people of enemy and enemy-occupied countries. The transmitters of ABSIE, BBC, "Voice of America" and United Nations Radio, AFHQ were linked in this world-wide network, which was beamed toward the European continent.

As time went on, strategic propaganda material which fell into the hands of PWD/SHAEF from its normal intelligence sources or from psychological warfare reporters in the field with the Armies, was channeled by PWD back to the strategic radio with suggestions for its use. Special recorded material was made at the front and this passed through PWD/SHAEF (Main) destined for the civilian agencies. Special directives covering the wishes of the Supreme Commander relative to the use of strategic radio beamed to the people in the areas under his control were channeled through PWD to the civilian agencies involved.

III. Operation of Mobile Transmitters in Liberated Areas

The one outstanding example of this kind of PWD work took place at Cherbourg immediately after the fall of that city late in June 1944. This operation was begun by personnel of the Second MRBC attached to First U.S. Army and was taken over by AIS, the consolidation field force of PWD/SHAEF. Briefly, the circumstances on the Cotentin peninsula were such that a certain amount of civilian confusion reigned as the result of the recent Allied landings; and it was deemed wise to use a Mobile 399 transmitter unit as a local voice to aid in reaching the people with Civil Affairs announcements and instructions. The transmitter was installed on the hill overlooking the city and although its range was not great, it was sufficient to reach the people of Cherbourg and vicinity. This new and temporary "Radio Cherbourg" relayed certain BBC and ABSIE programs during its two hours of broadcasting each evening and developed sufficient local features to win a valuably loyal audience for the more serious aspect of its work—which was to keep the people informed of their responsibilities as the first area of liberation in Western Europe.

Nowhere else in France did PWD (or its alter ego, AIS) operate such a transmitter as an Allied instrument for consolidation purposes.

IV. Operation of Public Address Units in Liberated Areas

This function, again, was more specifically one of Allied Information Service (AIS) rather than PWD proper, but since the overall operation of public address units was a responsibility of the Radio Section of PWD/SHAEF, a description of this work is included here, rather than in a later chapter which will describe the work of AIS.

The dividing line between the use of public address units in combat and in consolidation operations is extremely hazy. In almost all instances public address units attached to Armies performed the primary consolidation work. Because of their mobility, they could move quickly into a liberated town and without further ado give the people their first hard news of the progress of the fighting beyond, of the details of their own liberation, and what Civil Affairs wanted them to do. After this first stage, however, when the public address units of the Armies moved on, the consolidation work by public address units became the responsibility of SHAEF'S AIS/PWD. This work continued on a larger and more regular basis the original work of the Army units. In certain areas, such as in Normandy, electric power failures often at least temporarily cut into radio listening. By the same token, it was often impossible immediately to start newspapers. Thus, the mobile sound unit was the simplest and often the only contact between the military command and the people of a newly liberated area.

In certain instances Army psychological warfare personnel was detached for continued operation in the consolidation field, but this was merely an organizational convenience. Public address unit officers monitored the BBC and ABSIE and prepared short news scripts for their own localized broadcasts. They made as many as twenty towns and villages in the course of a day's run and their acceptance by the populace was immediate, continuing, and gratifyingly loyal. In general, sound truck consolidation operations continued in an area until the need for them was eliminated by the reappearance of newspapers and the reinauguration of radio listening.

V. Assistance to Liberated Areas

When Radio Cherbourg went on the air it was as an Allied station. There had been no "Radio Cherbourg" before the war. When Rennes was liberated, PWD engineering reconnaissance officers examined the transmitters and found that, although they had been damaged by the retreating enemy, they could be repaired. Orders were immediately dispatched to the United Kingdom for the stockpiled equipment that was needed. Meanwhile a mobile 1-kilowatt transmitter was used in Rennes and served in place of the damaged transmitters. Although the transmitter belonged to PWD, it was not operated as an Allied transmitter but as a purely French transmitter. PWD program and technical personnel did most of the work at the beginning and they were relieved one by one as the radio agency of the French government — Radio Difussion Francaise (RDF) — was able to supply replacements.

On a smaller scale, the same kind of assistance was given RDF in Paris. There the transmitters already were on the air under RDF management before the Germans were completely out of the city. However, certain equipment, musical recordings, and personnel assistance were required and PWD supplied them.

VI. Operation of Captured Static Transmitter
(Radio Luxembourg)

The most important single operation of the Radio Section PWD/SHAEF was that involving "Radio Luxembourg". This powerful 150 kilowatt transmitter, which was one of the most important pre-war transmitters in all of Europe, fell to the Allies in the Autumn of 1944.

Because of the importance of this operation, a detailed account of the background will be given here.

Before September 1939 Radio Luxembourg had been operated by a private commercial company, which had built the station under a franchise contract from the Luxembourg government. The Government received annual royalties from the operating company. Unlike nearly all other transmitters in Europe, Radio Luxembourg had engaged in commercial broadcasting.

On September 1, 1939, the Luxembourg government required the transmitter to go off the air in order to avoid possible charges by the Germans of breaches of neutrality. In May 1940, the Germans occupied Luxembourg and took possession of the station. From then until September 1944 the Germans used Radio Luxembourg as a major outlet for their propaganda network. They employed many of the Luxembourg civilian technicians who were familiar with the station. Several, however, refused to work for the Germans and were of extreme value to the Allies when Radio Luxembourg finally fell into our hands.

Meanwhile, in May 1944 the Luxembourg Government in Exile in London delivered to PWD/SHAEF a letter authorizing the Supreme Commander to take over and utilize Radio Luxembourg as long as it should be required by the military situation.

On the morning of September 1, 1944, when American forces were approximately 100 kilometres from Luxembourg, the Germans blew up the main control room in the basement of the studio building of Radio Luxembourg and began to dismantle certain of the instruments. German transmissions over Radio Luxembourg ceased on that day and most of the German civilians evacuated the transmitter site at Junglinster without damaging it, leaving a skeleton guard. One of the Luxembourg civilian technicians who had refused to work for the Germans, entered the studio premises and the transmitter and found the former empty and the latter undamaged. However, he learned that it was the plan of the Germans to blow up the transmitter before the American forces arrived. He was able to persuade the German chief engineer, who was still on the premises, that damage should be limited to destruction of the tubes, on the ground that this would be sufficient to prevent transmission for at least six months. The German engineer agreed and between September 1 and the arrival of the Americans this plan was carried out. All the tubes and other equipment were left in place. The glass portions of the largest tubes were broken, and the smaller tubes and a large stock of spares were punctured with bullets. No other damage was done. On the 9th of September, the loyal Luxembourg technician, Metty Felton, learned that some time previously a stock of spare tubes had been moved to the post office warehouses in Mersch for safety from air bombardment.

On September 10, elements of the Fifth Armored Division, First U.S. Army, arrived in Luxembourg City. An examination of the studio disclosed that there had been no damage beyond the explosion of September 1, although apparently preparations had been made for further destruction in the control room. Approximately 50 kilos of dynamite charges and 25 caps and fuses were removed from the control room. The Germans had removed some of the amplifiers from the studio control rooms, but nothing else. A large stock of phonograph records and an extensive music library were found. On September 11, Morris Pierce (OWI), a PWD radio engineer attached to Psychological Warfare Division, 12th Army Group, arrived in Luxembourg City. Felton undertook to guide him to the transmitter at Junglinster. It was learned that there were still Germans at the transmitter site. Pierce thereupon reported to Headquarters Fifth Armored Division where the Commanding General assigned a platoon of tanks and a detail of engineers to capture the transmitter. Early the next day the assigned force accompanied by Pierce proceeded to the transmitter, the approaches to which had been mined. One tank was blown up by a mine but there were no Germans at the transmitter. Felton learned that the stock of spare tubes at Mersch had been removed two weeks previously to Diekirch. On September 14 the stock of tubes, which was found to be intact, was removed to Junglinster.

As soon as the transmitter was taken, the Radio Program Production Unit of the Psychological Warfare Detachment, 12th Army Group began planning tactical programs directed against the enemy. On September 17, electric power was turned on at the transmitter and the carrier wave was put on the air for the first time. The next day, SHAEF began sending in operating personnel, with William H. Hale as Chief of the Station. On September 23, operation of the station was begun with relays from London and New York. The next day, 12th Army Group personnel produced four 15-minute programs which were to be continuing features of the station. These programs were tactical in nature, addressed to the German troops and to civilians in the immediate combat zone. The programs were: (1) "Story of the Day" based on front line intelligence, exposing weaknesses in units of the German Army facing the 12th Army Group; (2) "Letter Bag," consisting of captured German troop mail; (3) "Frontpost," carrying material from the small newspaper of that name distributed by air to the German troops; (4) a program of appeals to specific German units to encourage surrender.

In most of these programs use was also made of recordings from the field containing brief interviews with German prisoners of war and civilians.

On October 3, the Chief of Staff, SHAEF approved a directive placing the station under control of PWD/SHAEF for operation. This was based on the principle that although the transmitter was physically in the area of 12th Army Group, its signal was heard in the areas of all three Army Groups. Therefore, it was concluded that, for uniformity of guidance for output received by listeners over the entire area, especially in strategic broadcasts, policy and output should be under direct control of SHAEF. Programs later to be produced by SHAEF personnel were to be primarily strategic in nature, addressed to the German population behind the combat zone and ultimately to German civilians in occupied areas. All programs produced by 12th Army Group and, later, by the Luxembourg Government, were to be subject to approval by SHAEF its under policy guidance and directives.

On October 15, 1944 PWD/SHAEF designated the personnel assigned or attached for duty by it in connection with the operation of the station as "Radio Luxembourg Detachment of PWD/SHAEF." On October 23, Lt. Colonel Samuel R. Rosenbaum was designated as Commanding Officer, Radio Luxembourg Detachment of PWD/SHAEF. The 4th MRBC was designated to provide the required administrative and some of the technical personnel for the station. Personnel of Radio Luxembourg Detachment was attached to the 4th MRBC, for rations and quarters. The Detachment was authorized to employ local civilian help for necessary services to be paid out of funds available to PWD from the civilian agencies. Shortly thereafter such payment was made by the Luxembourg Government under Reverse Lend-Lease. On October 24, personnel made available by the BBC arrived to assist in preparation and production of SHAEF programs. At the same time, William H. Hale's designation was changed to Chief of Broadcasting.

Later in the month, PWD was authorized to set up a separate prisoner-of-war house at Luxembourg for German prisoners who had been screened to participate in psychological warfare broadcasts to Germany. This house was operated by the Radio Luxembourg Detachment for the joint use of 12th Army Group and SHAEF.

As noted in the chapter on the Intelligence Section, a subsection for intelligence was set up at Radio Luxembourg to control the flow and use of intelligence material received from SHAEF, Army Groups, and lower echelons.

The first daily SHAEF news program went on the air on November 10. It was given a distinctive musical theme chosen from the Nimrod Movement of Elgar's Engima Variations. This theme was used on all SHAEF news periods.

Through the following months, additional SHAEF programs of news and intelligence material were added to the expanding schedule.

Meanwhile, however, came the Rundstedt counter offensive. On December 17, word was received of the approach of German troops. At the direction of 12th Army Group, broadcasting from Radio Luxembourg was suspended at 2100 hours on December 19, when the enemy was in force a few kilometers from the transmitter site. Certain essential parts of the transmitter were removed and transported to Verdun. Preparations were made to evacuate the studio building. Fortunately, the military situation improved and the transmitter was reassembled in time to resume broadcasts at 2300 hours on December 23. Special Christmas programs designed for Christmas Eve and Christmas Day were produced in full.

On January 6, 1945, Noel F. Newsome (BBC) replaced Mr. Hale as Chief of Broadcasting. He served in this capacity until his resignation in May 1945, when the duties of Chief of Broadcasting were assigned to the Commanding Officer of the station.

During January 1945 Luxembourg City was under intermittent German fire from small rocket bombs. The studio buildings were not hit, however.

Until November 15, 1944 Radio Luxembourg was on the air for a total of $11 1/4$ hours per day, including seven relays from New York, twenty-three relays from BBC and four relays from ABSIE. Thereafter, operating hours were changed to a total of twelve hours per day with twelve relays from New York, and seventeen relays from BBC. Later, the relay schedule was reduced still further and more locally-initiated programs substituted.

As from April 1945, Radio Luxembourg supplied short-wave to OWI-New York a total of between 5,000 and 10,000 words per day of news, special events, and intelligence. These consisted of four-minute live inserts for the New York German, Polish, French, and English programs. For BBC, an average of 30 minutes per day of material was prepared at Radio Luxembourg and recorded. The recordings were sent via courier to Paris, where they were relayed to BBC. This material was primarily for use by the German Section of the European Service of the BBC.

Several hours per day of operation of the Radio Luxembourg short wave transmitter were placed at the disposal of PRD, 12th Army Group for transmitting news and talks to the American press and radio networks.

On March 27, 1945, the first special program of news and comment produced by 21st Army Group was presented by a group of British officers sent from the Army Group Headquarters. These programs were presented thrice weekly, emphasizing news from the 21st Army Group front.

The format of the SHAEF news programs on Radio Luxembourg was approximately one-third war news from the Western and other fronts, one-third special intelligence items from occupied and unoccupied Germany, and one-third a talk or commentary by war correspondents.

Sources of material for the news portions of these programs were partly the news files of the established commercial agencies and partly the special files distributed by PWD/SHAEF (Rear). These were monitored and received by Morse monitors at the station. In addition, certain English, French, and German voice transmissions were monitored for additional material.

All material submitted for output was reviewed and checked for compliance with SHAEF policy directives and guidance by the Chief of Broadcasting, or his Deputy, at the station, who were directly responsible to PWD. No material of any kind was broadcast without receiving stamped approval for security clearance by the field censorship unit stationed at the studio. This consisted of a group of field censors from 12th Army Group, operating under guidance and stops received through the field censorship service from SHAEF, Army Groups, and lower echelons.

The programs addressed to foreign workers in Germany were constructed to approximately the same format as the SHAEF news programs, except that they emphasized news and intelligence of interest to their special audiences in each language and the commentary emphasized instructions and suggestions to foreign workers in accordance with SHAEF policies. Such programs to foreign workers were broadcast from Radio Luxembourg in German, French, Flemish, Dutch, Polish, Italian, English, Czech, and Russian. The programs for Belgian and for French workers were produced by official representatives of the respective governments attached to Radio Luxembourg. The remaining programs were produced by U. S. or British personnel assisted by local civilians.

These programs had the distinctive musical theme known as "The Song of the Trojan Horse." Interviews with liberated foreign workers testifield that this theme came to be recognized by listeners all over western Germany.

From the commencement of operation in September, music was used throughout the program schedule to give variety to programs and to hold the attention of the listening audience. At first, such music was produced entirely from recordings. From 24 October 1944 the music periods were carefully organized each to have a separate character, including a nightly 45-minute Symphony Concert. There was also a relay of High Mass from the Luxembourg Cathedral every Sunday morning and a weekly organ recital from the Cathedral by the Cathedral organist.

Special emphasis in the music programs was given to music by composers banned by the Nazis.

From time to time special services were rendered by Radio Luxembourg to the Supreme Commander on request. These included the broadcasts of proclamations and instructions issued from Supreme Headquarters to German troops and civilians in Germany in connection with combat operations, as well as "The Voice of SHAEF" and "The Voice of Military Government" carried by other Allied transmitters.

Attached as an appendix to this paper is a detailed report on PWD/SHAEF technical radio work prior to the surrender of the German Army.

VII. LEAFLETS

I. Background

The largest single operation of PWD/SHAEF against the enemy was in the field of leaflets—largest, that is, in terms of continuing day by day tasks and in day by day production of materials.

As was noted earlier in this paper, large scale leaflet operations directed to the people of enemy and enemy-occupied countries had been going on since the beginning of the war. These operations had been conducted by PID and OWI separately, although a certain amount of coordination had taken place. There was also cooperation relative to use of printing facilities in the United Kingdom. Very soon after America's entry into the war it was recognized by OWI that it was impossible to produce leaflets, or other airborne printed material, in America for dissemination over the continent, simply because of the time lag necessitated by transport difficulties. Consequently, throughout the year 1943, OWI brought numerous personnel to London to enlarge the scope of its leaflets operations based on Britain. By the time PWD/SHAEF came into existence early in 1944, OWI leaflet operations on the American side already had progressed to the point where a squadron of B-17s of the 8th Air Force was occupied exclusively in leaflet dissemination.

On the British side, the RAF continued to disseminate large numbers of British leaflets nightly.

The first step toward PWD coordination of the British and American leaflet efforts was in the establishment of a joint layout, printing, and production section to serve PID and OWI. Personnel from PID and OWI were supplied to fulfill the various posts in this section. By May of 1945, when Germany surrendered, and leaflet operations as such came to an end, the Anglo-American leaflet operation was utilizing exclusively more than 80% of the total offset printing capacity of the United Kingdom.

Leaflets, as a weapon of psychological warfare, have a long history. They simply represent a written message from the commander of one force to a particular audience on the other side. In their simplest form they might be handwritten. The Colonial Forces utilized leaflets in the American Revolutionary War. These were directed against the Hessian mercenaries serving with the British Forces and urged them to desert and to take up land in the New World as their reward.

In the final months of World War I, the effect of Allied leaflets directed against German troops is strongly underlined in the memoirs of Hindenburg and Ludendorff.

By the beginning of World War II, much that had been learned in the field of leaflets had been forgotten. This was true both concerning the correct psychological warfare approach and methods of dissemination. During World War I, leaflets had been disseminated in certain instances by artillery. The French, for instance, used an adaptation of their 15 mm shell. The Americans used the Stokes mortar. This entire artillery technique had to be relearned in World War II. However, aircraft were available in World War II to an extent undreamed of in World War I. Thus, from the beginning, the RAF carried leaflets with each load of bombs dropped on the Reich. During the first winter of World War II — the so-called "phony war" period — hundreds of thousands of

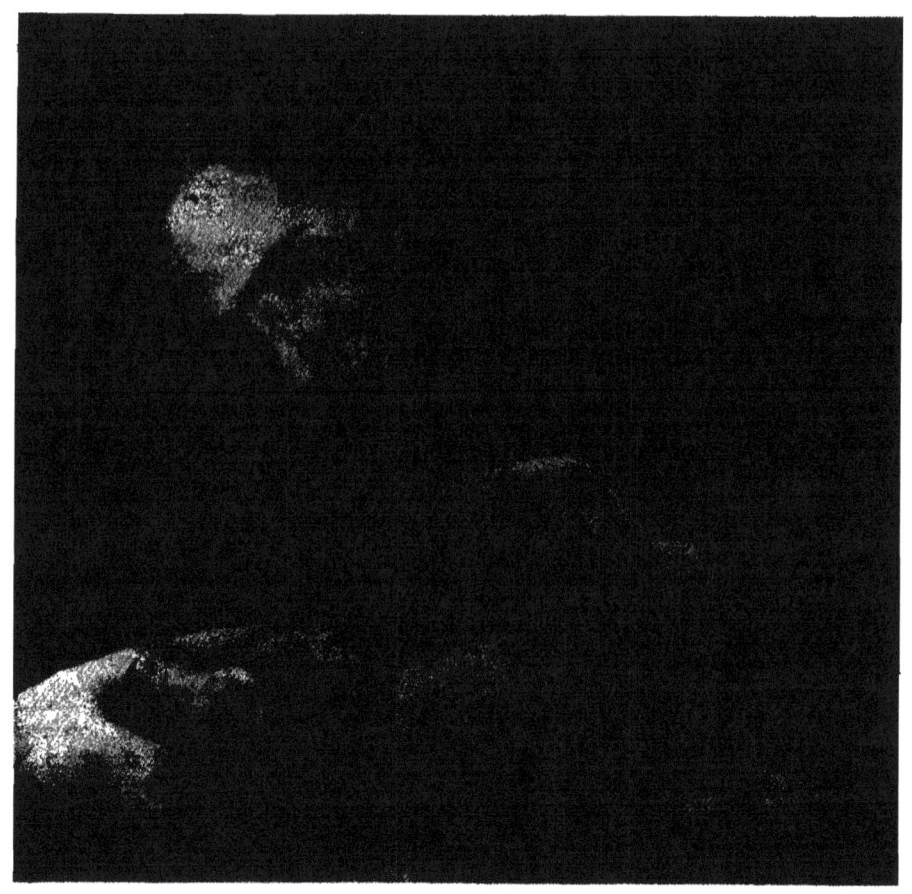

Maj. (then captain) James Monroe, AC, adjusts the fuse on a leaflet "bomb." Maj. Monroe, assigned to PWD/SHAEF, was largely responsible for the development of the bomb which permitted extremely accurate leaflet coverage of desired areas from B-17s.

leaflets were dropped on Germany with, of course, no noticeable effect. The time and circumstances simply were not ripe for psychological warfare. The technique of dropping leaflets from aircraft during this period was primitive. The leaflets were tied in small bundles and dropped out of the aircraft. Later, leaflets were placed on the bomb-bay doors in such a way that they were released as the doors were opened and the leaflets fluttered down from the bombing altitude.

This method produced area coverage but no accuracy. It was estimated at one time that with this method of dissemination an average of about 4% of leaflets dropped at any time actually found their way into the hands of the population to which they were directed—and that of the 4% many were gathered by "leaflet hunting expeditions" into rural areas near the target cities. In 1943 parallel experiments were going on in the United Kingdom and in AFHQ, aimed toward the development of a device which would control the dissemination of leaflets and limit their coverage to a target area. Out of these experiments came the so-called leaflet bomb. The one which finally came to be used exclusively by the special bomb squadron of the 8th Air Force — the 422nd — was the result of work by Major James Monroe of PWD/SHAEF and is called the Monroe Leaflet Bomb. A description of this bomb will be found at the end of this part of the paper.

II. Kinds of Leaflets

As the techniques of leaflet writing and dissemination were sharpened by experience, standardization of leaflet sizes came as a natural corouary. Experimentation showed that a leaflet, whose dimensions were approximately 5" by 8", could be packed into leaflet bombs or leaflet shells. A single sheet leaflet of this size came to be known as a leaflet unit and larger leaflets were based on this original size. Thus, a single leaflet of two pages, each 5" by 8", was known for statistical purposes as two leaflet units.

From beginning to end of the leaflet operation, various kinds of leaflets were used. One-shot leaflets bearing a specific message were a basic ingredient in the entire program. However, they were not the most important of the leaflets disseminated from the United Kingdom. As early as 1942, both OWI and PID inaugurated airborne newspapers. The first of these was a PID production called "COURIER DE L'AIR," which was followed soon by a similar American airborne newspaper called "L'AMERIQUE EN GUERRE." These were weeklies. Each represented four leaflet units and were designed to keep the people of occupied France informed of the progress of the Allies. Later, a similar airborne newspaper, called "STERNENBANNER" was disseminated in Germany. Others were produced for the people of other occupied countries. Later still, not long before D-Day, a daily paper called "NACHRICHTEN FUR DIE TRUPPE" was produced for the troops of German garrisons along the Atlantic Wall. This, incidentally, was an example of gray propaganda, in that its source was not indicated. In the other airbone newspapers, the source—the British or American governments or the Allied Forces—was clearly indicated.

Beginning some weeks after D-Day, the basic leaflet used by PWD against the enemy was the Passierschein—SAFE conduct pass—which bore the authenticating signature of the Supreme Allied Commander and gave German soldiers instructions on how to surrender. In some cases the reverse side of the leaflet bore an immediate tactical message or important news item.

In general, no PWD leaflet or leaflet-type message was argumentative in character. Wheter it was an airborne newspaper or a single-shot leaflet, its approach was objective and its content factual.

As in the field of radio, leaflets throughout the campaign recognized two audiences, namely, friends and enemies. Airborne newspapers, such as L'AMERIQUE EN GUERRE, brought news to people of friendly occupied countries; and instruction leaflets brought to them the details of what the Supreme Commander wanted them to do in such circumstances as the actual invasion of Normandy and, farther eastward, in the face of the approach of the Allied Armies.

Relative to the enemy, PWD addressed German troops and German civilians in the light of the differing conditions between them. As time went on, PWD also addressed the millions of foreign workers and prisoners of war in Germany. This was particularly true in the weeks preceding the final German surrender, when the Supreme Commander had specific intentions concerning the movement or non-movement of these people. In the course of the piece-meal liberation of Displaced Persons in Germany, PWD assumed the task of assisting G-5 in repatriation. This function took the primary form of an airborne four-language newspaper, called "SHAEF," which transmitted the Supreme Commander's instructions to the various nationalities of Displaced Persons in Germany. A more complete description of this function will be found in a later chapter. The airborne newspaper "SHAEF" was similar in format to "NACHRICHTEN," which it gradually replaced in the few weeks predecing surrender and in the months thereafter. "NACHRICHTEN" and "SHAEF" ran four pages. "NACHRICHTEN" appeared in two editions consisting of between 750,000 and 1,000,000 copies each. Like "SHAEF" it was distributed every night when flying was possible. "SHAEF" achieved a maximum circulation of about 2,000,000 daily before the need for it began to decline. After the German surrender the method of disseminating "SHAEF" was changed. Bundles of copies were parachuted on predetermined targets, where they were picked up and distributed by G-5 to the Displaced Persons' camps.

III. Writing and Production of Leaflets.

The physical task of writing leaflets was in point of fact probably the smallest part of this vast operation. In general, leaflets bear little text. However, the concentrated mental effort of producing regularly, month by month, new texts to fulfill immediate and potential needs was great indeed. Leaflet writing was done by the language regions in OWI and PID and by several officers attached to the PWD Leaflet Section. Leaflet writing was done in consultation with PWD deputies, members of the Plans and Directives Section, members of the Leaflet Section, and the PWD G-2 and G-3 liaison officers. The daily production of such continuing items as "NACHRICHTEN" and "SHAEF" was done by a staff at PID.

There can be little descriptive material on the general subject of how to write a leaflet. Basically it is a matter of keeping aware of the changing military situation, the situation as regards the morale of the Wehrmacht or of the particular audience contemplated, of production schedules and—perhaps most important of all—of the overall policy which covered PWD's work. This policy, as has been stated before, was to represent as clearly and as firmly as possible the hard news of the military situation and the wishes of the Supreme Commander; the latter always was based on the former.

When a leaflet text was approved, layout and production men from the Joint Production Section quickly put the material into work, aiming at deadlines which varied with the circumstances.

The Leaflet Section maintained continuing liaison with those sections of the Air Forces which carried out the dissemination.

IV. Dissemination

Through the agency of the special leaflet squadron, approximately 80% of all leaflets disseminated in the areas of the Anglo-American armies was by the 8th Air Force. Approximately 10% was done by the RAF, approximately 5% by the fighter bombers of the Tactical Air Forces, and approximately 5% by artillery.

The fighter bombers came into the leaflet picture after the use of the leaflet squadron had become more or less a matter of routine. Psychological Warfare Detachments with Armies gave the coordinates of desired targets to Air Force liaison officers who made contact with the bombers commands. A special bomb was developed for leaflet dissemination by fighter bombers and this is described at the end of this section.

As noted earlier, Psychological Warfare Detachments of Armies and Army Groups produced many of their own leaflets for artillery dissemination. Many others, however, were produced by the PWD/SHAEF Leaflet Section on request from Army and Army Group teams and shipped, already rolled, for insertion into artillery shells. At the end of this section will be found a description of the methods used in artillery dissemination.

V. Statistics

Between D-Day and the German surrender, PWD disseminated, or supervised the dissemination of, more than three billion leaflets.

VI. Leaflet Bombs

In December 1943, the 422nd Bomb Squadron of the 8th U.S. Air Force for the first time demonstrated graphically the urgent need of an accurate device for the dissemination of leaflets by air. On this occasion the leaflets were released from huge boxes in the bomb-bay of a B-17 flying at 30,000 feet. In order to allow for the 60 mile per hour winds that existed at that altitude, it was necessary to release the leaflets over Brussels in order to have them land somewhere near Paris, which was the target. The boxes used for this mission (and for successive missions prior to April 19, 1944) were converted luggage carriers obtained from the Air Transport Command.

These boxes were hinged on the bottom and could be released by the same mechanism used to release the bombs from the bomb-bay. The smallest quantity of leaflets of the standard size that could be released at one time was about 350,000, one half of the bomb bay. This gave rise to a great waste of paper, effort, and time, for there were few localities within range of the Fortresses which could effectively absorb this large quantity—if the release were correct and leaflets landed, in a concentration.

An aneroid device, designed to open the bundles of leaflets at altitudes below flight level, was tried at this time. These "Aneroids" had small levers, to which the cord binding the packages of leaflets was tied. In theory, as the packages fell downward, the barometric pressure acting on the aneroid canister would compress the canister, overcome the binding strength of the cord's pull, and trip the release of the levers, allowing the binding cord to fall free of the package. The mechanism was not successful because the aneroids were expected to do more work than they could perform, since the release of the tightly bound package required a force much greater than the 32 pounds per square inch which atmospheric pressure exerts at sea level. Efforts at loosening the cord and thereby decreasing the pressure required to release it were not satisfactory because this left the packages insecurely wrapped. In this condition, the packages would break up and disseminate as soon as they fell into the slipstream of the aircraft. (It was found that few square shaped packages—unless they were sealed complete—could withstand the terrific force applied to them by the slipstream from an aircraft flying at speeds greater than 150 MPH. Most aircraft which are operated at altitudes above 25,000 feet fly at speeds in excess of 225 MPH.)

In December, the 8th Air Force designated the 422nd Squadron of the 305th Bomb Group, which had been flying operationally at night since July, to drop leaflets only as directed by OWI. Thus, coordination of writing and dissemination was possible for the first time on large scale operations. The one remaining problem was the inaccuracy of the leafleting. Members of the Squadron attacked that problem with enthusiasm.

The first effort at producing a leaflet bomb, which the Squadron suggested, was a modified Lindhom Dinghy container. This modification proved to be such a difficult job that the suggestion was refused. Shortly afterward, Headquarters, USSTAF began receiving large quantities of M-17 chemical bombs, which were packed in a shipping carton with ideal specifications. The container, without modification, could be efficiently fitted into the bomb bays of American combat aircraft, since it was of approximately the same diameter as the 500-pound demolition bomb. By a very simple process, a fuse, fin, and bursting charge could be added in order to control the flight of the "bomb" after release. This device could not produce "precision" leafleting, but would remove most of the doubts surrounding the release of leaflets from aircraft by fixing the maximum inaccuracy at 5 miles in average winds.

On the 4th of February, 1944, the first "bomb" test was conducted over The Wash in England. The cardboard M-17 containers, packed with leaflets and equipped with a mechanical time fuse were released from 10,000 feet. Containers, $17^{1}/_{2}$" diameter and 47" in length, held approximately 80,000 leaflets 4.5"×8.25". A Fortress could easily carry ten such bombs after carrying-lugs had been added, thereby increasing the normal load of the Fort from about 70,000 leaflet units to 80,000 units. The fuse of the bomb was set to detonate five seconds after release. An observer aircraft was sent along beneath the releasing aircraft at the altitude which it was believed the bomb would burst, that is 4,000 feet below.

The folowing observations were made on the first release:
1. Complete detonation occurred 1,000 feet below the aircraft.
2. The setting of the fuse (5 seconds) was accurate.
3. The bomb tumbled twice before detonation.
4. Dissemination was instantaneous, beginning first with a very closely-grouped concentration of leaflets, then gradually "fanning out" until it was estimated that the dispersion of leaflets falling in normal 10 to 12 MPH winds for 5,000 feet would cover roughly one-half to one square mile in a fairly heavy concentration.
5. The bomb casing disappeared entirely after the explosion, satisfying the requirement that no falling particles cause injury or damage to people. or property of occupied countries.

From these observations it was concluded that the bomb was a vast improvement in the technique of leafleting. The case was both simply and easily manufactured, packed and released. Although it was evident that it was necessary to obtain more information regarding the time of fall of the bomb, and more conclusive information regarding the dispersion of the leaflets after bursting, it was decided to begin production of the item immediately in the UK for use by the Special Squadron and the daylight bombers of the 8th AF.

Plans and specifications of the test bomb were given to the Ordnance Officer of USSTAF with a request to establish the modification depot necessary to produce 1,000 bombs per month. The depot was established in Bedfordshire. The first completed products of the depot were used on May 16, 1944 and were used consistently thereafter. There was one major modification: the shortage of supply of the M-111 fuse forced the utilization of the M-860 barometric fuse, which was manufactured with a pre-determined bursting altitude. This caused several difficulties.

In order to be able to maintain a well dispersed, yet concentrated pattern of leaflets, the bombs must be at the same altitude above the target. This necessitated the stocking of several series of the barometric fuse so that there would always be a suitable item for use in releasing over mountainous regions or over plains.

The use of the barometric fuse, though extremely simple for the bombardier and navigator in setting up their bombing problem, gave rise to certain malfunctions. Since the nose of the T-1 bomb (as the modified container came to be known) was not streamlined, it was believed that a pressure area was produced on this flat surface as the bomb fell earthward after release. This air pressure was in such a place as to assimilate barometric pressure on the mechanism within the fuse, and many times caused the premature detonation of the fuse by compressing the aneroid cannister and releasing the firing pin of the fuse. The air vents on the outside of the fuse were large enough to allow a sufficient quantity of air flowing at a great enough velocity to actuate the mechanism. Tests were conducted constantly to try either to perfect the fuse by removing this possibility of malfunction, or by adapting another fuse which could not be affected by erratic weather conditions or momentary flight circumstances.

Following the first few missions conducted by the Special Leafleting Squadron, the practicability of the use of leaflet bombs on the daylight missions of the 8th and 9th Air Forces became evident. USSTAF directed that aircraft loaded with leaflets be dispatched with each mission conducted over Germany itself. Now that bombs could be used, there was no danger to other aircraft of the formation, and the leaflets would fall into the area bombed.

This technique was highly successful until, as the plans for the invasion of the continent progressed, it became necessary to coordinate very carefully the location of the targets in Germany with the military plans and with the content of the leaflets. At this point in the development, a psychological warfare "team" was established at 8th Air Force Headquarters to supervise distribution by taking the maximum advantage of air lift available. This air lift was provided by an additional directive from USSTAF, dated June 21. The directive stated that on each daylight bombing mission six groups—two in each of the three divisions of the 8th Air Force—would furnish two aircraft each loaded with leaflets. This system proved successful, since liaison with the Plans and Directives and the Intelligence Sections of PWD could best be coordinated with the A-3 and A-2 of the Air Force by such an establishment. No opportunity for coverage was missed in this way, and operation could be conducted with a minimum of inconvenience to the Air Forces.

The fighter bomber operation was conceived by Wing Commander Price of the Leaflet Section, who attempted on March 9, 1944 to adapt the 250-pound target indicator bomb used by the RAF as a leaflet bomb. First tests indicated that though the bomb was successful as a dissemination device its modification was not practical. Tests, conducted later with the American M-26 flare container, were successful; and it was adopted immediately. The modifications that were necessary were not extensive and could be made in a very short time.

The M-26 container (when modified it became known as the Mark II Nickol bomb. The American designation was the T-3 Propaganda bomb) was 37" in length and could be loaded with approximately 14,000 leaflets of the standard unit size made from 22 pound stock. The main difference between dissemination by the T-1 and the T-3 was that the pattern of leaflets on the ground from a T-3 formed a cone. The average length of this cone is approximately 300 feet. Leaflets from the T-1 fell roughly into a circular pattern on the ground covering between one-half square mile and one square mile.

The T-3 bomb could be clustered on all of the standard fighters, which meant that the fighter-bomber on a leaflet mission could carry between 28,000 and 84,000 leaflets, all of which, when released carefully by the pilot, could be placed on an enemy concentration up to company strength, assuring that leaflets would be easily seen by all members of the company. With the knowledge that this pin point accuracy existed, the use of the fighter-bomber as a medium for dissemination of leaflets was easily justified.

In conclusion, it must be stated that very little information is available about the effects of convection current on free fall leaflets. Since aircraft flies at high altitude (or if at low altitude, at high speed) there is little opportunity to observe the fall of leaflets after dissemination has occurred. Therefore, we do not know the effects of extreme temperatures, rough terrain, thermae currents produced by isolated bodies of water and land on the velocity and direction of the fall of the leaflets.

VII. Leaflet Shells

For dissemination by artillery, leaflets were rolled for insertion into the shell. When the 105 mm. shell was used (cavity dimensions $11^{7}/_{16}$" in length, 3" diameter) two rolls of the standard size leaflet, both rolled on the short axis were used, with cardboard washers as separators. Each roll contained about 250 leaflet units, totalling 500 for a single shell. The 155 mm. shell carried approximately 1500 leaflets. There was little use made of the 155 mm. shell for leaflet purposes during the European campaign.

The following procedure was most often followed in modifying the 105 mm. Howitzer smoke shell M-84 for use:

a) All ammunition was removed from cases and projectile removed from fiber case. The propellant remained in its fibre case at all times, whether it was issued in a separate or same fiber case. All projectiles were stacked sideways, and fiber cases and top covers kept separate from the projectile during the modification process.

b) Personnel engaged in the preparation of rounds found that the most efficient working method was to employ a small workbench approximately 2' high and 4' long. The round was placed sideways on the flat surface of the bench, with the man straddling the bench at one end.

c) Holding the round with one hand, a spanner wrench was used to unscrew the base plate which had a left-hand thread. (The spanner wrench was specially for this purpose. It consisted of a steel bar approximately 12" in length, one inch in width, and $1/_{4}$" in thickness. At one end two small lugs, $2^{1}/_{2}$" apart, were built in the steel bar protruding not more than a $1/_{4}$". These two lugs fit into two hole recessers in the bottom of the smoke shellbase plate.)

d) After the base plate was removed, the contents of the shell, consisting of one copper sealing disc, three HC smoke canisters, three to six cardboard washers, a metal baffle plate, and a small black powder charge were extracted.

e) The powder charge was replaced in the cavity in the nose of the shell and the metal baffle plate reinserted, insuring that it was seated flatly and squarely on the shoulders of the recess chambers.

f) All base plates and sealing discs were stacked at one side and all canisters placed in heavy box for later disposal.

g) The empty shell then was picked up by another man and seated, nose down, in a rack which consisted of a wooden or metal box 4' long, 3' wide, and 1' high, on whose top approximately 20 holes 4" in diameter had been drilled. All shells were held in place by this rack. A third man inserted the required number of cardboard discs, insuring that they were flatly seated next to the baffle plate.

h) After all protective cardboard discs had been inserted, the rolls of leaflets, separated by a cardboard disc, were inserted, insuring first that the gummed paper holding the roll together was cut. The leaflets were rolled clockwise from the center out.

i) The remaining space in the shell then was filled with cardboard washers until the sealing disc just failed to seat against the rear face of its recess.

j) The base plate was screwed home until flush with the end of the shell.

k) The loaded round was then immediately placed in its cardboard fiber case and the case stencilled with the designation number given to the leaflet.

l) It was found desirable to insert one copy each of the German-English translation of the leaflet in the cardboard case before replacing the top. This served to make it possible to determine quickly the text of the leaflet in the round.

m) All HC canisters removed from the shells were turned in to the salvage section of the Army ammunition depot or Corps ASP's.

n) All leaflet-loaded ammunition was delivered to the ASP's or artillery units in their fiber cases. These cases sufficiently protected the projectile from inclement weather for extended periods of time.

The 155 mm. shell was issued without fuse and without propellant charge. Fuses were drawn separately either by PW personnel or by the using artillery unit. In the event the M 67 fuse was desired, this was drawn at the depot specifying its proper nomenclature, which was TM 67 fuse, modified for use in base ejection smoke shells. A limited quantity of these modified fuses were usually available at Army ammunition depots but it was found advisable to arrange a continuous flow of this fuse through the Army Ordnance Officer.

The modification method of the 155 mm. shell for use with leaflets was identical to that of the 105 mm., the only difference being, aside from its larger size, that a fourth, coneshaped canister was used in the 155 mm. The overall cavity dimensions of the shell from baffle plate to bottom of base plate was $18^{1}/_{2}$" in length with a diameter of $4^{3}/_{8}$". Because of the tapering effect of the fourth canister which fitted in the nose of the shell, it was found most expedient to leave this fourth canister in the shell and utilize only the remaining cavity which was $14^{1}/_{2}$". Cardboard washers were placed on top of this fourth canister for protection against the powder charge flame and two large rolls of leaflets, not exceeding $4^{3}/_{8}$" in diameter, were inserted in the shell. The balance of loading was performed as in the 105 mm.

VIII. SPECIAL OPERATIONS

In its earliest beginnings Allied psychological warfare was waged—if so vigorous a verb may properly be used—in an almost complete vacuum. That is, radio broadcasts were initiated and leaflets written and disseminated with no more than the most shadowy association with the military operational planning of which they were presumed to form a part.

As time went on and the possible psychological warfare contributions to military success came to be recognised in AFHQ and in certain Allied black propaganda operations initiated in the United Kingdom, psychological warfare increasingly was put into the overall military operational planning picture. Thus, by the time of D-Day, PWD/SHAEF liaison officers were sitting regularly with G-3, SHAEF and PWD was called upon to submit formal staff studies and other recommendations concerning the possible part that psychological warfare could play in forthcoming Special Operations.

Psychological warfare's part in the total sum of SHAEF Special Operations naturally varied greatly with the type of operation. In some, because of their nature, PWD's recommendations concerning its own possible contribution were negative. In some few others, as the operations finally shook down, psychological warfare was the only weapon used. It must be stated that in these latter cases, almost without exception, failure was the result, proving again the early axiom that psychological warfare can seldom be successful without a show of military force.

The development of the Allied campaign after D-Day, when viewed from the standpoint of psychological warfare, reveals the increasing integration of PWD into the total SHAEF staff planning organism—the ultimate result of gradually increased understanding of the sharpened techniques and more nearly measurable results to be obtained from intelligent use of this newest and hitherto least understood weapon of total war.

In the following pages will be described the part that the Psychological Warfare Division of Supreme Headquarters played in some typical Special Operations.

The media for covert propaganda during Operation "OVERLORD" have been four. (1) a combined radio program of news and music for the German Armed Forces known as "Soldatensender Calais" and "Kurzwellensender Atlantik" broadcast daily; (2) a daily newspaper dropped by American aircraft; (3) talks for the opposition movement within the SS; (4) leaflets distributed in occupied countries and Germany aiming at undermining pro-Nazi morale. These operations were generally known as "black" propaganda.

Both before and after D-Day the main tone of black propaganda was to concentrate the attention of the German soldier on the enemy within his own ranks, i. e., Nazi Party authorities rather than on the enemy without.

In the strictly military field it was endeavored to keep before the mind of the soldier in the West the military disasters on the Eastern Front, the weakness of German war production under the stress of Allied bombing, the impotence of the Luftwaffe, and the breakdown of German police authority.

Prisoners of war captured during operations on the Continent stated that the Calais transmissions were heard by them regularly and most of the contents believed. Special success was achieved by the campaign representing the

Generals' conspiracy on Hitler's life as a powerful movement to save Germany from military disaster.

"Huguenot"

One of the Special Operations—code named "HUGUENOT"—was a plan conceived with the idea of undermining the efficiency of the German Air Force by suggesting to the Luftwaffe authorities that German flying personnel are deserting in their machines to the Allied side. The method contemplated was to provide the German Air Force commanders with evidence indicating desertion with Allied connivance by regular hints and stories appearing on their desks in the monitoring of wireless output.

The dividends from this operation were expected not so much in the actual number of desertions as in the effect of the countermeasures which the German authorities would be induced to take against the flying personnel if they were deceived in believing that an increasing number of them were deserting.

The measures expected to be taken by the German authorities to prevent desertion were: the sharpening-up of anti-desertion measures and instructions to field police to keep a suspicious eye on everyone—a course which would have serious effects on morale. Also, the promotion of officers on account of political reliabiliy rather than efficiency.

"Nest Egg"

During the fight for Brittany, PWD drew up a psychological warfare plan to accelerate the surrender of the Channel Islands after August 20. The military situation was such that there was no assault force available to fight for the islands.

The operation—called "NEST EGG"—intended to use a captured German General to make contact with the Commanding General of the German Channel Islands garrison to induce him to surrender. Failing that, it was proposed to open up a leaflet and radio attack, with the primary object of informing the troops of their situation, and secondly, weakening their morale to a point where a demonstration of air strength might be sufficient to induce surrender. This was to be done by dropping the German soldiers' newspaper "Nachrichten."

When, on September 22, 1944, contact with the Islands' garrison failed to result in a surrender and showed no demoralization of the troops' morale, it was decided that no further psychological warfare attempts would be made and that the nightly air dropping of leaflets on the Channel Islands would be discontinued.

This proved unmistakably that psychological warfare as an adjunct to military operations could succeed only when the position of the opponent is a hopeless one and when he has realized the futility of holding out any further.

"Braddock II"

This operation was directed at the millions of foreign workers in Germany who, it was felt, constituted a potential internal threat to German security. It was a scheme for dropping from the air about four or five million small, powerful time fuse incendiaries on concentrations of foreign workers in Germany and Austria for use by them against suggested targets. Attached to each incendiary was a card containing instructions "how to use" in nine languages. Each package of incendiary contained a folder mentioning likely targets.

It was expected that if the foreign workers would use the incendiaries, it would have not only the desired sabotage results, but also the result of straining to the utmost the enemy's security precautions.

After the liberation of Paris, it was believed at Supreme Headquarters that military operations had developed to a point where foreign workers should make their maximum contribution. As a result, in mid-September, leaflets were dropped by Allied aircraft on German territory calling upon the foreign workers to make their contribution to liberation by making full use of instructions and materials (Braddocks) dropped to them for sabotage. This call to arms was followed up by the Allied Calais Radio on its nightly broadcasts. The appeal in the leaflet was made over the signature of General Eisenhower.

By monitoring the German radio and by means of reports from neutral capitals (Stockholm and Berne) it was established that the appeal considerably disturbed and confounded Nazi officials and that German newspaper and radio comment had been equally jittery.

During the early months of 1945, when military operations did not augur a quick conclusion of the war, the use of (Braddocks) was considered as being of only morale value; the sabotage angle was discontinued. A series of small drops were, therefore, made over a long period of time with the object of stretching the German security service by keeping them in a constant state of apprehension and watchfulness.

In late April these operations were discontinued, when, with the advance of the Allied land armies deep into the heart of Germany, it became increasingly evident that the war would soon come to an end.

"Clarion"

Another example of the combining of psychological warfare and actual military operations was Operation "CLARION." The plan called for extended intensive attacks by the Allied Air Forces against the German transportation system (to begin in January of 1945) to bring about a disruption of rail and water lines of communication, thereby aiding the American and British ground forces. In addition, the attacks were expected to force the enemy to resort to motor transportation to carry out high priority movement, thereby depleting his carefully conserved petroleum products.

To implement this vast operation by psychological warfare, Brigadier General McClure recommended to the Commanding General of the United States Strategic Air Forces in Europe that the use of propaganda be made a part of the plan and coordinated with the actual bombings.

Specifically, the General planned that once the operation had commenced, news of its effects would be played up heavily to the German people—by Allied broadcasts and other means— and especially to railway workers, telling them to stay away from their jobs if they wish to save themselves from harm. Broadcasts to German troops at the front was to stress the fact that as a result of the bombings, they were isolated from their bases and supplies. The weapon of psychological warfare was here to be utilized to drive the morale of Germans down to the lowest possible levels when still under the stunning blows of the air offensive and to prevent it from emerging from that state.

"Capricorn"

Commenced in the last week of February 1945, this operation had as its objective the undermining of German morale by propaganda talks, based on actual as well as spurious intelligence, proving that Germany has already lost the war and that to continue to fight would only mean to aid in the destruction of German life and economy.

A speaker, in military tone and by dint of his inside information, purported to represent an underground movement within Germany advocated, amongst other things, the immediate overthrow of Hitlerism as Germany's real enemy and the acceptance of surrender terms as the only way to avoid annihilation of the German nation.

In support of this "black" undertaking, the use of "white" leaflets, produced by the United States Office of War Information, were resorted to. The reasoning behind the use of this "white"—or overt—propaganda was that Germany could be blanketed with material dropped from planes suggesting that the Allies have heard this station within Germany, agree with its output, and encourage the German people to listen to a voice coming from within.

"Aspidistra"

Operations that played havoc with the German people's morale in the last months of the war, and just about finished off their endurance, were intruder operations conducted on the Cologne, Frankfurt, Berlin and Hamburg frequencies of the German Home Service in March 1945, with the object of spreading confusion in the German administrative plan.

These operations—break-ins on the German medium wave radio programs by Allied commentators speaking in German with false news reports—made it very difficult, if not impossible, for the German listener to sift the true from the false.

In addition, the Allied transmitter used to beak in on the German news periods with cleverly disguised orders from the Gauleitung, which started considerable unrest. This form of wireless propaganda broadcasts, by the announcement of the approach of Allied tanks, evacuation orders, etc. not infrequently created chaos in the German transport system.

IX. ALLIED INFORMATION SERVICE

As has been seen, the primary responsibility of PWD was to assist the fighting arms and branches in defeating the enemy. Thus, psychological warfare directed against German troops and, secondarily, against the German home front constituted PWD's first task. Important too, however, was PWD's consolidation function to the extent that it could aid the military command in securing and maintaining lines of communication through liberated areas.

The first stage of consolidation work was done by personnel from Army combat teams. This necessarily was restricted to a very brief period of time since this personnel was required for continuing combat propaganda functions farther forward. Thus, it devolved upon PWD/SHAEF to provide a field force to conduct continuing consolidation functions on the continent in the rear of the Forces. Like so many other aspects of PWD work, the task of consolidation in Western Europe was without clear precedent.

PWB in North Africa had conducted little consolidation propaganda. The primary function of PWB in North Africa was to conduct psychological warfare against the enemy, either while he was still in Tunisia or when the fighting had crossed the Mediterranean to Sicily and Italy. PWB/AFHQ did conduct large scale consolidation operations in Sicily and Italy, but it was done among people who were not officially Allies. In Western Europe, on the other hand, PWD's consolidation activities were to take place among people who were distinctly Allies and beyond this, in the case of France, people for whom the populations of Britain and America entertained a strong personal feeling of friendliness and sympathy. In such a situation PWD had to be prepared to operate with a degree of diplomacy not hitherto required.

To fulfill the need for such consolidation operations among friendly populations, a subsidiary of PWD, called the Allied Information Service, was established. The elimination of the phrase Psychological Warfare from the title was done simply because it did not appear to be diplomatic to speak in terms of "waging psychological warfare" against our friends.

AIS was made up of a Group Headquarters, designated the 6805th AIS Group Hqs. (Prov.), and, at the beginning, three field teams each with a commanding officer.

AIS Group Hqs., together with certain personnel designated as Advance PWD/SHAEF and the personnel of the first field consolidation team, landed on the Normandy beaches July 5, 1944 and reached Cherbourg the following day. In the original planning AIS was to operate behind rear Army boundaries.

However, even after the liberation of Cherbourg, rear boundaries of the Anglo-American Forces in the field still were on the coast of France. Negotiations were continued between AIS and the Publicity and Psychological Warfare Branch of the First U.S. Army and the original interdict against operations by AIS forward of rear Army boundaries was lifted. A line was drawn across the Cotentin Peninsula, roughly half way between its base and its tip. Personnel from the First U.S. Army combat propaganda team which had inaugurated consolidation operations in Cherbourg, the first sizeable city of France to be liberated, was withdrawn and personnel of the first AIS Consolidation Team (the 6806th AIS Field Consolidation Team [Prov.]) took up the tasks. Within a few days First U.S. Army's P & PW Branch requested that AIS Publications and

Cinema Sections operate forward of the demarcation line that had been drawn across the peninsula.

As will be noted in the several sections on media operations in this account, combat propaganda personnel had initiated publication of the Cherbourg newspaper, established the radio station and had reopened cinema theaters.

It was such functions as these that AIS continued and exanded.

Following the Allied breakthrough at St. Lo, the area for AIS operations suddenly expanded. Cinema and publications operations in particular grew to large proportions almost over night. Personnel, which at the beginning had been super-abundant because of the resticted area of operations granted AIS, rapidly became too small to cover the area that fell to it. In succession, the first team which had taken up duties in Cherbourg moved to Rennes, and the second team (the 6807th AIS Field Consolidation Team [Prov.]) took up duties in Cherbourg. With the passing of the weeks, the three teams (including the 6808th AIS Field Consolidation Team [Prov.]) were headquartered at Cherbourg, Rennes, Le Mans and Reims.

Selected personnel from the Advance SHAEF Group, from AIS Group Hqs., and from the teams joined the P & PW Section of 12th Army Group Task Force to enter Paris. This Task Force entered the city on liberation day, August 25 and immediately began setting up headquarters not only for itself but in preparation for the imminent arrival of PWD/SHAEF (Main). Billets and offices were requisitioned and a mess established.

Meanwhile, as is shown in the sections on the several media, AIS operational personnel began the work of centralizing in Paris those operations which had been begun in Normandy and Brittany.

Intelligence officers covered the liberated areas of France and, as a by-product of their work, collected vast amounts of primary evidence of German atrocities in France, which later were made available to interested sections of SHAEF.

The missions of AIS had been stated before D-Day as:

a. To aid the Allied military effort by helping to insure that the populations of zones in rear of Armies were kept aware of the degree and nature of cooperation required of them, and by endeavoring to counter rumors that might breed panic.

b. To render necessary aid to the liberated governments in reconstituting their public information media—such aid to include services, personnel, advice, and equipment.

c. To remain as anonymous as possible while helping the liberated governments to help themselves.

d. To bring about its own dissolution as early as practicable.

In support of (d) above, AIS was prepared to dissolve itself as of October 15, 1944, some seven weeks after AIS entered Paris. The plan had been that the information functions of AIS were to be turned over to the civilian information agencies of the British and American governments, namely, the Ministry of Information and the Office of War Information, respectively. These agencies were to perform their tasks on a national and civilian basis rather than, as with AIS, on a military and Anglo-American basis. With its own dissolution in view, AIS had called in the personnel of the three field consolidation teams in France and had billeted this personnel at a chateau near Paris. Here they were to be combed out, with part of the personnel to be earmarked for the forthcoming German operation and the rest returning to their respective agencies or units, whether civilian or military. However, AIS did not come to an end on October 15.

In late August and September the end of the war against Germany had appeared to be near. By mid-October it became obvious that another winter of the war loomed. Paris, instead of returning to its former place as the hub of a 'tightly organized system of communications, was in point of fact practically isolated from the provinces—isolated, that is, except for Anglo-American military transport. The food situation in France, primarily because of lack of internal transport, was deteriorating and the outlook for the winter was extremely dim. The disappointment over the failure of the Anglo-American Forces to end the war as quickly as the people of France had expected was one of the major factors which added up to a condition of badly depressed national morale.

This situation was compounded from the standpoint of informational activities by the fact that much of France still was a military zone in which the civilian information agencies could not function as such.

In view of all these circumstances, the decision was reached not to dissolve AIS but to order it to continue its activities so long as they should be needed. It was decided that, as circumstances permitted, one or another of the AIS functions should be turned over to the civilian agencies. Thus, through the winter of 1944-45 and the spring of 1945, AIS continued as an operating entity fulfilling what was a manifest need. It was in this situation, too, that Brigadier General McClure, Chief of PWD/SHAEF, ordered travelling pictorial exhibits to tour the provinces of France, an enterprise which is described under Publications and Display."

AIS finally and formally came to the end of its task as of May 1, 1945, when the last of its joint activities—publications—was turned over to the OWI and MOI.

In Belgium and Holland other PWD-AIS teams engaged in information activities similar to those of AIS in France. In Belgium and Holland they functioned under the SHAEF Missions to these governments.

In conclusion, it should be stated that one aspect did not, in fact, work out in practice. This was the concept of the Field Consolidation Team as a self-contained operating entity. The nature of the work, and the fact that the area of operations changed so radically and rapidly in the wake of military events, meant that rapid deployment of small groups of specialized personnel was necessary. In order to fulfill this need, AIS Group Headquarters was forced to assume greater and greater control of individual personnel within the teams to the end that AIS Group Headquarters eventually assumed complete operational control of that personnel rather than exercising it through the team leaders.

The Low Countries, Denmark und Norway

In the early planning for PWD/SHAEF in London, all of the occupied territories were included in a single overall plan. However, in operations after D-Day and until the end of PWD involvement in certain of the operations, consolidation activities in France were separated for purposes of convenience from those in the Low Countries, Denmark, and Norway. Particularly after PWD/SHAEF (Main) moved to Paris, joining AIS Headquarters which had preceded it there, consolidation activities in France fell, for all practical purposes, directly under AIS-PWD Headquarters. On the other hand, as time went on and territory was liberated, consolidation activities in the Low Countries were conducted on an increasingly detached basis. This work in the Low Countries was done through the SHAEF Military Missions to Belgium and the Netherlands.

Just as there had been an AIS Group Headquarters and three field consolidation teams for France, there was a similar set-up for the smaller Allied countries which were in the process of liberation. For these countries there was the so-called No. 1 Group Headquarters which administered three consolidation teams known as No. 12 PW Consolidation Team (for Belgium); No 10

PW Consolidation Team (for the Netherlands); and No. 11 PW Consolidation Team (for Denmark). The SHAEF Missions to the liberated countries were replicas of Supreme Headquarters in miniature. A Special Staff Section of each was the PW Section. The PW Consolidation Teams were attached to the psychological warfare representative on the Mission.

In order to facilitate control of consolidation activities on the continent, a so-called Liberated Areas Desk was established in PWD/SHAEF Headquarters, with representatives both at Main and at Rear—Main then being in Paris and Rear in London. This desk supervised consolidation activities in liberated areas, maintained liaison with the SHAEF Missions and with Special Force Headquarters (Norway) and was made responsible for the ultimate arrangements for handing over the PWD-AIS consolidation functions to the British and American civilian agencies when that time should come. The Liberated Areas Desk at PWD/SHAEF (Rear) was responsible for coordinating the flow of special equipment and supplies stockpiled by the civilian agencies in the United Kingdom for use in the Low Countries.

The liberation of Belgium followed the liberation of most of France; and in order to hold PWD consolidation personnel immediately available for use in Belgium, some of the teams came first to France and personnel was employed in the French operation awaiting the opening of Belgium. Thus, in every way, experience gained in France contributed largely to the success of consolidation operations later in Belgium and Holland.

Belgium

PWD exercised a supervisory authority over all consolidation activities in Belgium. The PW Section of the SHAEF Mission to Belgium was at first a sub-division of the Mission's G-2 and later a sub-division of the Mission's G-3.

A major task of PWD-AIS in Belgium was to assist in the rapid rehabilitation of the Belgian radio broadcasting system. Anglo-American radio technicians were sent direct to Belgium from the United Kingdom to undertake delivery and erection of transmitters which had been negotiated for months earlier between PWD/SHAEF and the Information Services of the Belgian Government in Exile.

Throughout the period of the operation, PWD assisted the Belgian Government in all aspects of this task. Recording trucks were provided as well as transmitter tubes and frequency crystals. Communications receivers were made available and advice was given on the design and erection of antennae. Interceded with SHAEF signals on allocation of frequencies and aided in obtaining power authorizations for the transmitters.

For the Belgian press, PWD provided a news file from London and assisted in arrangements for monitoring this file. A regular flow of news pictures was made available, as well as radio photo equipment. PWD assisted in solving transportation problems for the Belgian press and negotiated in the whole field of copyrights on features, news and cartoons. In the realm of publications and display, posters were made available to the Belgian Civil Affairs group and new posters were prepared on atrocities in Belgium and paying tribute to the Belgian aid to the Allies. Publications material was distributed on a basis similar to that of France. A travelling photo exhibit—again similar to those which toured France—opened first in Brussels and then proceeded to other important cities. As late as June 1945 the exhibit was drawing 25,000 visitors a day in the battered city of Antwerp. PWD also assisted in expediting the shipment of books and reference material into the country.

Holland

The circumstances of PWD Consolidation activities in Holland were similar to those in Belgium, the major difference being that it was not until late December 1944 that operations were possible and even as late as April 1945 only a part of the country was open.

Beyond this, PWD, functioning through the SHAEF Mission, provided goods and services in Holland as it had in Belgium, namely, engineering and other aid in radio; a news file; picture service; films; radio recordings; and radio communications receivers.

PWD arranged for the installation of broadcast transmitters at Maastricht, Eindhoven, Meppel, and Lopik/Jarrsveld.

Denmark

PWD operations in Denmark began May 12, 1945, after the surrender of the German forces in the country. There had been little or no material damage to facilities, and the PWD function was in the field of supplying information materials—newsreels, pictures, radio recordings, etc.

Norway

As in Denmark, PWD Consolidation activities in Norway did not begin until after the collapse of the Wehrmacht. By that time, plans had been formalized for assumption of informational tasks by the civilian agencies of the British and American governments. These agencies functioned through the appropriate embassies, but PWD representatives, attached to the SHAEF Mission, conducted Display exhibitions of the Allied military effort on a joint basis until arrangements were completed for assumption of the entire task on a civilian basis by the representatives of the State Department and the Foreign Office.

X. PUBLICATIONS AND DISPLAY

A. Publications

I. Introduction. As has been seen, the PWD Leaflet operation was almost exclusively a function of combat psychological warfare; that is, its objectives were enemy troops, enemy civilians, the people of friendly nations occupied by the enemy.

The PWD Publications operation on the other hand was primarily a consolidation function. Prior to the occupation of Germany, the PWD publications operation had as its objectives the people of liberated Allied countries.

Because of manifold problems of accounting, external and internal transport, and the sheer bulk of the material involved, the publications operation was among the most ramified in which PWD engaged.

Prior to the occupation of Germany, the areas in which the PWD Publications Sections functioned in the field came under the jurisdiction of the PWD subsidiary, the Allied Information Service, whose general activities have already been described.

Generally speaking, the PWD Publications operation can be divided into two parts, namely, (1) production and stockpiling, and (2) distribution.

II. Production and Stockpiling. Long before PWD/SHAEF came into being, the civilian agencies, OWI, PID and MOI, had begun the task of producing the stockpiling publications material for distribution in liberated Allied countries. Because of lack of adequate precedent for this kind of work, it must be stated that much of this early production was done in a haphazard way. In retrospect it would appear that too many non-recurring titles were produced and these in too small quantities for adequate coverage when liberation came; and the extreme desire of the people for non-collaborationist reading matter became apparent.

Certain of the material stockpiled for France had been designed originally for distribution in French North Africa. What had appeared to be adequate for Colonial France often was somewhat naive for Metropolitan France.

In any case, by the time the Publications Sections of PWD/SHAEF was set up early in 1944 in London, much of the original bulk of material for liberated Western Europe was either in production or already stockpiled by the civilian agencies. A Joint Publications Committee, made up of representatives of PWD, and the civilian agencies, was established to sit on suggested new items for stockpiling. At the same time, the PWD Publications Section studied the lists of available publications in the Western European languages to determine which of those already available should be used, which should be pulped, and which should be reprinted in larger quantities both in England and in America.

As a result of the early work by the civilian agencies, a total of 141 separate titles of non-recurring publications were prepared for France alone. As noted above, in most cases, these had been produced in insufficient quantities. The retrospective opinion of the PWD Publications Section was that a more efficient list would have contained but twenty or thirty items in much larger quantities.

It must be stated, however, that without the independent production by the several civilian agencies, haphazard though it was during the many months before the establishment of PWD, it is likely that D-Day would have found

PWD with a woefully insufficient total stockpile, even though the titles contained in that stockpile might have been more carefully chosen.

Publications produced and stockpiled after D-Day fell roughly into two categories, non-recurring items and periodicals. Generally speaking the periodicals were the more popular, but this may well have been due to the fact that they simply were pitched on a somewhat lower intellectual level. However, whether or not the fact that illustrated periodicals were the more popular constituted them the better propaganda medium appears to be debatable. Outstanding examples of the illustrated periodicals were VOIR on the American side and CADRAN on the British side. These appeared fortnightly on alternating weeks. They were roughly similar to PICTURE POST, LIFE, etc.

The selection of the non-recurring items—the one-shot publications—was an extremely difficult and ramified task. The problem was to view the history of the world and of the war during the four years of German occupation and somehow to synthetisize this vast accumulation of facts, ideas, and events for the benefit of people who had been living under conditions that approximated intellectual blackout. To make the problem even more difficult, the exact nature of this blackout was not known in Britain and America. Not until surveys could be made in liberated areas would planners be able to make even an approximate determination of how much these people knew and how much they were in ignorance.

It could, however, be determined beforehand that because they had access to the BBC and other Allied radio broadcasts, the occupied peoples of Western Europe had been kept fairly well abreast of the surface bulletin facts of the war. But they had no understanding of the true magnitude of the global war, nor of the Allied effort being expended to win it. Beyond all this there was the whole field of new economic and social ideas looking toward the world in which these liberated people would be called upon to play a part after the war. The complete outlines of post-war international thinking aimed toward joint security could not be given adequately in a radio bulletin. This kind of material, then, was to form a part of the publication stockpile for distribution in liberated areas.

A continuing discussion went on before D-Day concerning the mood and character of material which the liberated people would wish most to have. Should it be light and entertaining for people released from four years of occupation? Or should it be weighty in order to bring them quickly up to date on the important events that would affect their lives for years to come? The answer to these questions seems to have been found in VOIR and CADRAN on one hand, and in translations of Oxford pamphlets, and the like, on the other. Support for the philosophy that weighty but pertinent material would be needed had been available in the experience of PWB/AFHQ many months earlier. PWB Publications had found to its surprise that in southern Italy, in a notoriously unintellectual part of the world, a cheap newsprint edition of the Beveridge Plan was one of the most pupular items available to the people from PWB/AFHQ.

No hard and fast line could be drawn as between the one type of material and the other. Specific reader reaction came only with time in the months following D-Day. And if the titles had been selected haphazardly and if in retrospect there appeared to be many glaring holes in the total lists of publications available, it must be stated by way of mitigation that when finally the combined PWB-AIS Publications Section closed its books, there were no "returns" from dealers. The supply—good, bad and indifferent—was far exceeded by the demand for Allied reading matter.

III. Distribution of Publications. The task of distributing PWD. publications in the liberated countries of Western Europe was probably even more difficult and ramified than the job of producing those publications. Transport was the first problem—transport from the PWD base in the United Kingdom to the continent, and internal transport within the countries of Western Europe.

Again, to a certain extent PWD/SHAEF had a body of trial and error experience in PWB/AFHQ to draw upon. In the early months of PWB/AFHQ in North Africa, publications were distributed free of charge to the people. This was done through the medium of so-called Propaganda Shops, which were opened in larger cities. Interested citizens could go to these shops, select their publications, and carry them away. This was haphazard in the extreme. Often children obtained publications simply as collector's curios. There was no efficient method of insuring equitable coverage among people who were really interested.

On the basis of this experience PWB/Italy decided to distribute publications on a commercial basis, thereby making it worth the while of professional newsdealers to trade in these publications. This meant, of course, that the Anglo-American governments would be placing a price charge on their output. Previous to this departure, the British and American Treasuries had not been in the habit of taking in monies from such sources. However, favorable rulings were obtained and for the first time Anglo-American publications began to obtain some degree of effective and measurable coverage of the audiences intended.

Discussions on the whole problem of sale of publications went on in London prior to the establishment of a similar policy for PWD/SHAEF operations on the continent. For France, the largest and most important area of potential liberation, it was planned to utilize the distribution facilities of Messageries Hachette, the publications distribution monopoly which had functioned in France before the war and during the occupation. The problem of dealing with a monopoly was discussed and it was decided that in the absence of any other means of distribution PWD must deal with the monopoly. However, it was planned to so draw contracts with Hachette that PWD would be free to deal with other agencies if such should become established.

All titles planned for distribution in liberated countries were cleared prior to D-Day with representatives of the several national governments in London or Algiers, and all PWD plans for distribution were discussed with members of the several Ministries of Information involved.

The first publications-distribution team, a part of AIS, arrived in Cherbourg on July 6. It brought with it a one-ton truckload of publications. Actual operation began on July 10 when these publications were placed on sale in Cherbourg.

The following procedure was inaugurated in Cherbourg and continued throughout France:

Upon entering a new locality the team member first contacted the highest local French authority. In regional centres, such as Toulouse, this would be either the Regional Delegate of the French Ministry of Information, the Commissaire General de la République (those were direct representatives of the De Gaulle Government superimposed upon the regions) or the Prefect, depending upon who was present. If more than one were present, all were contacted.

In small localities, contact was made with either an Assistant Regional Delegate of the French Ministry of Information or, if one was not appointed, the Mayor. The purpose was explained to him and his cooperation requested in the designation of a local dealer of clean political record who was equipped to handle the material. In the great majority of cases, this was the local representative of the Messageries Hachette. In a few instances, the Hachette dealer was found undesirable because of collaboration, in which case, another dealer was found. After designation by the French authorities, a visit was made to the local Civil Affairs officer who was informed of the details and his confirmation requested.

A previously prepared form was then signed by the four parties: the French authority, Civil Affairs, the AIS representative, and the dealer. This procedure was uniformly successful.

Allied interests were protected and any dispute could be referred to a responsible authority. Four cases arose wherein the official appointee appeared to be unpopular with the public. The case was immediately referred to the French authority who arranged the affair satisfactorily.

After designation, a contract form was signed with the dealer giving the precise terms and discount rate. Next, investigation was made of the capabilities of the dealer to distribute our publications, his pre-war circulation ascertained, and estimate made of his sales possibility.

In many cases his shop had been destroyed or partially demaged by the war In such instances, Civil Affairs was asked to aid in requisitioning and furnishing a new place of business. Requisitions for gasoline for the dealer's use also were frequently obtained in the same manner. There is no record of any abuses of these requisitions.

Normal distribution through Hachette, Paris, to the provinces became effective in February 1945.

In the Normandy campaign, most small towns were serviced directly by truck or jeep delivery from Cherbourg. The opening of new territory made such blanket coverage impossible with the available personnel and transport. Arrangements were then made with dealers in key centers for distribution outward from those points. In Rennes, arrangements were made with the Rennes newspaper to carry publications with newspaper deliveries into the Brittany peninsula.

Eventually all departmental centers in France were put on a similar footing. Army gasoline allocations, when obtainable, were useful. Lateral train service remained in operation in the Toulouse and Bordeaux areas and was used by dealers for distribution outward from these points.

In normal times, Hachette serviced the smallest and largest of its representtatives directly from Paris. The dealer in Lyon serviced only the city of Lyon itself. AIS arrangements thus made unaccustomed demands on these local dealers for storage space, labor and transport, but in the majority of cases they were cooperative, and provided as efficient distribution as conditions would permit.

The first shipments of publications material from London were made in sample or "formula" packages. These were of approximately 80 lbs. weight and contained 10 to 27 copies of approximately 24 equally mixed British and American publications.

An initial delivery of these packages provided variety in the newsstand display. However, since some items sold more rapidly than others, the result was that dealers were often hesitant to take new sample packages when certain publications from previous packs were slow in selling. The small quantities of each item made it difficult to estimate the sale potential of a particular item.

The arrival of periodicals and other publications in bulk alleviated this situation, and formula packages were discontinued.

When Paris was liberated on August 25, 1944, a member of the publicationsdistribution team of AIS entered the city with the T-Force. Commercial contracts for distribution of material were drawn up with the French Ministry of Information and with representatives of the central headquarters of Hachette. Three tons of material arrived by truck from Cherbourg on September 2 and this was immediately put on sale in the Paris kiosks.

As time went on, more publications distribution personnel arrived in Paris and was headquartered there. With the opening of new territory, team members were dispatched on reconnaissance missions, signing preliminary contracts and making initial commission arrangements. During the month of September, Beauvais, Rheims, Chalon-sur-Marne, Nancy, Amiens and Troyes were serviced. In October, AIS serviced Lille, Angers, Lyons, Grenoble, Poitiers, Toulouse and Marseilles. All these deliveries were effected by organic transport. In November, sub-depots were set up in Lyons and Marseilles.

Until February 1945, the Paris-Hachette serviced only the city itself. As rail transport conditions improved, arrangements were made with French government officials for rail priorities which permitted Hachette to begin distribution in the provinces. By April 1 Hachette was in a position to take over all distribution.

Between July 10, 1944, when the first material went on sale in Cherbourg, and April 16, 1945, 15,758,893 publications items were distributed in France for total net receipts of 61,585,560.42 francs (approximately $ 1,231,711).

Publications were a tiny and relatively unimportant part of the total bulk of Army material loaded on the beaches of Normandy. Difficulties experienced in the initial phase of the operation at Cherbourg and dating up to the first three months of the Paris operation prior to the opening of the port at Rouen, may be traced to the following factors:

a) Both PWD and AIS were unfamiliar names to the Army personnel on the beaches. The beach area on which material was temporarily stored was 40 miles long and approximately 10 miles deep. Within these 400 square miles, specific areas were assigned to the different regular units of the Army Engineers, Medical Corps, etc. PWD-AIS material came under none of these categories and was therefore subject to dispersal, even of the same shipment, to widely separated points where it was again received as unfamiliar. There was consequent difficulty in trucking it to the warehouse. The eventual familiarity of the port authorities with PWD markings cleared the situation considerably.

b) At the beginning of the operation in Cherbourg, the Chief of the Shipping and Warehousing Section of AIS was seriously handicapped by lack of personnel. As material came in on the beaches it was physically impossible for him to run the Cherbourg warehouse which handled all AIS equipment as well as publications, and keep in adequate touch with the beach situation. In addition, the sorting and tallying of publications which arrived from the beaches in a jumbled state was a complicated task which demanded more time and manpower than was available. Sufficient transport was not available to move the material which soon began to arrive in substantial quantities. The arrival in the warehouse of 15 enlisted men in late July and additional transport carried by the second, third and fourth teams, alleviated the situation at Cherbourg. However, as the push toward Paris developed it was necessary for this Section to establish depots at forward points such as Caen, Rennes and Le Mans. No warehousing personnel was available. Publications team members accomplished the warehousing tasks at a sacrifice to their efficiency as distributing agents. The back log of this situation continued to be felt for the remainder of the year.

c) The warehouse tally-in and tally-out of approximately 200 different publications items titled in French was unfamiliar work to the assigned enlisted men. Engaged in a commercial transaction which demanded an accurate accounting of material, the lack of professional warehousing experience caused considerable difficulties necessitating constant readjustment in the business channels. As the enlisted personnnel gained experience, these difficulties lessened.

d) In the first stages of the operation, the label markings were small, unclear, and referred to the contents solely as "printed matter." Ensuing difficulties were:
1. illegibility after the rough beach handling.
2. confusion as to destination.
3. confusion as to contents requiring opening of packages for verification and consequent delay in delivery to agents.

e) Beach conditions were aggravated in the autumn of 1944 by the usual channel storms and heavy rains. Mud on the beaches caused transport delay, rendered labels illegible and caused loss of material. After the closing of the beaches, effort was made in December to clear publications material from the remaining stockpiles. A report of December 31, 1944 listed 10.7% loss of the material shipped to Cherbourg and various small ports on the Contentin peninsula. However, material continued to filter in. The final loss on all shipments from London up to April 16, 1943 by air, to Rouen, to Cherbourg, and to the beaches, was 2.4%. This improvement was the result of the concerted efforts of the PWD Shipping and Transport Section to locate material on the beaches, careful sorting out of good copies in damaged packages, and general tightening up of accounting records.

The PWD-AIS transport demands caused by the rapid liberation of the greater part of France after the fall of Paris caused withdrawal for other uses of part of the transport originally assigned to publications, and resulted in an arrangement with the Shipping and Transport Section of PWD, whereby all heavy transport of publications to key points was done by them. Each truck or convoy was accompanied by a Publications representative whose task it was to check tally-ins and conclude financial arrangements with the dealer. One panel truck remained for use of the Publications Section in Paris for specific rush assignments. One $1^{1/2}$ ton truck was assigned to the Lyons depot for the same purpose. Four jeeps were used for deliveries of small quantities of publications within the Paris area, field reconnaissance trips, and in the collection of accounts in the provinces.

Motor transport difficulties encountered may be traced to one or more of the following factors:

a) The enormous demand for publications after the fall of Paris, and the great number of thickly populated districts to be serviced, rendered the hitherto normal delivery of one $2^{1/2}$ ton truckload to be insufficient to the demand. At this time, PWD S & T Section had available from ten to fifteen $2^{1/2}$ ton trucks. Several times this number would have been required to deliver the publication stocked in warehouses and to have satisfied adequately the public demand over the large area.

b) PWD S & T Section was engaged in hauling publications from the beaches and the port of Rouen as well as delivering publications out of the warehouse to dealers. In addition, they handled the transport and warehousing of all other PWD supplies, radio equipment and leaflets. The delivery of leaflets to airfields, paper stocks for the manufacture of leaflets, and the hauling of indicated material arriving in the port had a higher priority than publications. For this reason, at certain periods, publications distribution was seriously curtailed.

c) The large territory south of the Loire river and west of the Rhone river contained no U. S. Army installations. Deliveries to this region were only possible by carrying adequate reserves of gasoline and food for the entire journey. Forty jerricans were necessary for the Paris-Bordeaux run. The space required to carry these cut heavily into the number of publications delivered.

B. Display

An integral part of the Publications Section's planned work was the whole field of display in liberated areas. This meant posters, news photographs and formal photographic exhibits. During the early months of the campaign in Northwestern Europe, however, this aspect of the task was dormant, primarily because of lack of qualified personnel and the pressure of the primary task of distributing publications.

In the early weeks in Normandy, to be sure, certain posters prepared before D-Day in the United Kingdom were distributed. These met with a mixed reaction, however, and relatively little effort was expended on them. A total of fifteen posters had been designed and executed by the OWI-PID Joint Production Unit in London and print orders had run from 25,000 to 75,000. After the initial mixed reaction to certain of the posters, the policy was laid down that posters would not be put up indiscriminately but would be given to any individual who asked for them, as well as to town mayors in small quantities for whatever display the mayors saw fit.

Informal window displays of news photographs were put up in various towns and cities in Normandy and Brittany, and while these attracted great interest, the true importance of the formal photographic display was not apparent until after the liberation of Paris.

Immediately after the arrival of the PWD T-Force in Paris on August 25, the showroom on the ground floor of No. 17 Boulevard des Capucines (on the Place de l'Opera) was requisitioned. Early in October the first formal display of war photographs was planned. A display architect was lifted from the United Kingdom, and work was begun on the manufacture of panels and other display requirements.

The exhibition opened with a preview for the French press on October 19 and for the general public on October 20. The exhibition contained approximately 250 photographs covering the Anglo-American war effort from the Battle of Britain to the fall of Paris, including sections on Pearl Harbor, the Pacific campaigns, the war in Russia, production, Lend-Lease, etc. The showroom accommodated no more than 3,000 visitors per day but a capacity crowd attended seven days a week until the show was closed on December 24, 1944. The total attendance was 204,578. Special visits were arranged for Paris school children and the French public reaction was one of extreme interest.

The morale of the people of France was at a dangerously low ebb in the autumn of 1944. Absence of adequate communications and transport left many parts of the country virtually isolated. Failure of the Allies to end the war soon after the liberation of Paris caused keen disappointment throughout the country. The passage of the Allied armies through France had been so rapid that large segments of the population had no understanding of the magnitude of the war effort.

In order to alleviate this situation somewhat, the Chief of PWD, in view of the unqualified success of the Paris photographic exhibit, ordered that seven similar displays be prepared and sent to tour the provinces. Anglo-American field personnel was recruited in Paris and London, and Publications reprensentatives made preparatory contracts in their respective regions.

The first travelling display opened in Toulouse on December 20, 1944. Another opened in Lyons on December 23. Successive exhibits opened in Bordeaux, Limoges, Marseilles, Lille, and Tours. After display in the major centers for varying periods, the exhibits moved on to smaller towns in the various regions. The final show closed in Montpellier on April 5, 1945. The following is a list of the cities covered: Lille, Roubaix, Tourcoing, Arras, Amiens, Rouen, Poitiers, Reims, Troyes, Nancy, Metz, Dijon, Besançon, Rennes, Redon, Nantes, Angers, Le Mans, Tours, Angoulême, Bourdeaux, Bayonne, Vichy, Limoges, Clermont-Ferrand, Lyon, St. Etienne, Grenoble, Perigueux, Cahors, Montauban, Albi, Auch, Toulouse, Pau, Tarbes, Carcassone, Perpignan, Montpellier, Marseille, Aix-en-Provence, Toulon, Nice.

The exhibit consisted of 60 panels carrying 200 photos. These panels were made of plywood painted in different light shades and were supported by detachable iron legs. Cases were made with slots for each panel and the whole was designed to fit a standard 2½ ton U.S. Army (6×6) truck. A tool kit was provided as well as pots of prepared paints and flags of the United Nations.

As a whole, the panels stood up well under the hard usage. Some difficulties were experienced with warping and the poor quality of paste available in France caused peeling of photos where they were exposed to the sun.

Posters announcing the exhibit, but with space for place and date left free, were printed in London and carried with the displays.

The teams consisted of two men, one British and one American officer (military or civilian). Withdrawal of personnel, as PWD teams for Germany were activated, eventually reduced the teams to one man each. These men made all contacts with French officials, found suitable locations, arranged for publicity, contacted the Press, mounted and dismounted the panels, arranged the decorations (procured potted plants, etc.) of the showroom, gave an official "vin d'honneur" to local officials, and remained in attendance at the exhibit to answer the public's questions. On accasion they were aided in these activities by help furnished by the Delegate of the French Ministry of Information, the Prefect, or other local officials.

The MOI and OWI prepared documentary material on the British and American war efforts which was offered to the local Press. Sample pulications and news photos from the Publications operation were given to interested individuals.

The official openings were attented by Army, civic and religious notables of the city. Speeches were exchanged at the "vin d'honneur" given afterwards, and photos taken on the occasion were given good coverage in the local press. In many cities, military bands and parades preceded the opening, with presentation of arms between French and American or British guards of honor.

The warmest receptions were encountered in the smaller cities, where the opening of the exhibit occasioned public holidays and where official contact with the Allied Forces was more rare.

In the three months' duration of the displays, the attendance records totaled 6,800,000. Assuming, as was often the case, that some persons came more than once, a conservative estimate is that five million people saw the displays. It was impossible to cover all the interested communities in the time allotted.

After the termination of the exhibits, many letters expressing disappointment were received.

Urgent requests were received from field men for an illustrated bookled reproducing the display and this was produced in London. Delivery of 50,000 copies came too late to be used in any but the Rennes, Le Mans and Rouen displays. However, sale of the booklet was an effective means of making the impact of the exhibit more permanent.

XI. PRESS

A. Press in Liberated Areas

The line of demarcation beween PWD press activities before the occupation of Germany and afterward was probably more sharply drawn than in any other medium in which PWD was involved. PWD press activity in liberated Allied countries, which was accomplished under AIS, took the form of aid to local entrepreneurs. PWD/AIS remained anonymous and restricted itself to supplying newsprint, temporary personnel, and radio receivers for access to wireless transmission and news.

In Germany, on the other hand, PWD's function, as will be seen in later chapters describing the entire information control activity, was a completely restrictive one of control under the military command in occupation.

The first free newspapers in Western Europe were published by members of the psychological warfare combat teams with the British and American armies soon after D-Day. These were at Bayeux and Isigny. These newspapers fulfilled an immediate need for information by people recently liberated. They were not, however, full scale newspapers in the accepted sense. They were more in the form of simple news sheets.

The first full scale daily newspaper was published in Cherbourg and appeared on the streets several days after the city fell to the troops of the American First Army. Pressure from the initiative of a member of the First Army Psychological Warfare team was responsible for the appearance of the paper. He stirred the local publisher from lethargy, took the lead in repairing those parts of the plant which had been destroyed by military action and supervised the publishing of the first issue.

A few days later, this officer was transferred temporarily to AIS, which by then had arrived on the continent, and the continued publication of LA PRESSE CHERBOURGOISE was accomplished with the aid of AIS. As time went, on this aid took the form of simply supplying newsprint, news pictures, and a special feature and news articles. With the paper on its feet, AIS interest continued because the paper constituted the most regular means of reaching the people of the Cherbourg area with Civil Affairs announcements, etc. As more of the Cotentin Peninsula was liberated AIS transport was utilized to distribute copies of the paper in the areas immediately in the rear of Armies. When the liberated area had become so large that full copies of LA PRESSE could no longer be delivered, AIS Press Section produced a wall news bulletin, a few copies only of which were distributed in newly liberated towns and villages where they were posted in the public squares.

After the experience in Cherbourg, AIS was called upon to assist but little in the reconstitution of French newspapers. When Paris was liberated, no less than fourteen newspapers, all of them without collaborationist taint, were already being published in the city.

Thus, the PWD/AIS press function was reduced to its simplest terms, namely, distribution of newsprint. From its own standpoint, however, as opposed to that of the French publishers, the AIS press function continued, with distribution of special articles which the military command or AIS itself deemed advisable in the context becauuse of the local morale situation.

In the early days after the liberation of Paris, AIS Press Officers dealt with the local newspapers in conducting such campaigns as those for the retrieving of jerricans and for combatting black market operations by the American troops and Parisiens. Although communications were difficult, AIS press officers also attempted to service the provincial press with similar articles.

The aim was to acquaint the people of France with the facts of the magnitude of the global war and beyond that, the part which Frenchmen could and must play in bringing it to a successful conclusion.

B. News

In support of all PWD activities on the continent, a News Division had been established before D-Day in London. The aim of this News Division was to provide by radio a file of world news, synthesized from all available official and commercial sources. The plan was sound but, unfortunately, it did not fulfill expectations in practice for a number of reasons. The primary reason, perhaps, was that transmitter power and broadcast frequencies made available to the News Division for transmitting its file were never equal to the task. Seldom was it possible to monitor this daily news file regularly and with ease. On the other hand, clandestine journalists in the occupied countries had learned during the occupation to monitor certain BBC transmissions for their news. When, after liberation, many of these journalists ceased to be clandestine and took over overt publishing missions, the habit formed during the occupation proved too strong and they continued to monitor the BBC rather than switch over to the PWD news file. The only real argument against this was that PWD news file aimed to synthesize Anglo-American news whereas the BBC was naturally heavy with British news.

In conjunction with the Directives Section of PWD, the News Division also broadcast each day a special brief transmission by voice known as the "Spider. This simply was a short commentary-like talk which, according to the order of the items discussed and the relative emphasis given to them, gave field teams guidance on the handling of the day's news.

For German newspapers, both those produced overtly under Allied military direction and by publishers licensed by PWD, a new agency was established in London, replacing the PWD News Division. This was known as the Allied Press Service and much of the personnel was the same as that which had staffed the PWD News Division. The Allied Press service produced a regular file of synthesized world news for transmission by radio to be monitored by PWD teams in the field.

XII. CINEMA

Experience in North Africa and Italy had proved—if, in fact, the point needed proving—that among the most popular effective means of public information is the cinema. From the very first days of the Normandy campaign, this was proved again. In Paris, almost the first question asked by the people after the liberation of the city was: When will the cinemas reopen? When shall we see "Gone With The Wind"?

The experience of North Africa and Italy had been sufficient to support long and serious planning with PWD/SHAEF for its cinema operation. Arrangements were made with the British and American commercial film producers for a stockpile of feature length entertainment films suitable for use in the liberated countries of Western Europe. In addition, feature length and short documentary films produced by the British, American, and Russian governments were stockpiled. Some of these films were supplied with foreign language sound tracks. For the rest, foreign language sub-titles were dubbed in.

In general, the stockpile of films available was not all that PWD might have desired. Certain entertainment films, for which a great demand developed, were not made available by the commercial producing companies.

The first full scale cinema show after Normandy D-Day was given in Cherbourg on the night of July 4, 1944, less than a week after the city was liberated. The feature of this performance was the British film "Victory in the Desert." There was also a newsreel. This newsreel was produced in London on a weekly basis and contained material of American, British, and French character.

It was learned early that no aspect of consolidation propaganda work was so important as the reopening of cinemas. The very act of reopening the theaters and permitting large groups of citizens to congregate in them for normal amusement purposes was in itself an important indication that a semblance at least of normality had returned. AIS/PWD attempted always to reopen cinemas as early after the liberation of a city as the military exigencies and electric power situation permitted.

Like publications distribution, the distribution of films was done by AIS on a commercial basis, under percentage agreements reached with the civilian agencies, OWI and MOI, and by them with the producing companies. As the area of AIS operations expanded, the cinema distribution section reopened the prewar decentralized film exchanges throughout the liberated areas and used them—often with their prewar personnel—in the normal way. Again, like the publications distribution experience, AIS Cinema Section was called upon to provide most of the transport for films by the exchanges and cities within their orbits.

Because of the nature of the cinema, little transport was required. A jeep-load of films tins represented weeks of entertainment and information for many cities. By the same token, and because sufficient experienced prewar cinema distribution personnel was available, the problem of accounting for funds on a professional basis was not a difficult one.

In addition to the regular commercial exhibition of films in established theaters, AIS operated several mobile cinema units. These units travelled the countryside, giving shows in isolated villages which did not have theaters or in towns where the theaters had been destroyed or where electric power was not available from mains. Upon occasion, AIS provided mobile power generators to service undamaged theaters in towns without power.

AIS also undertook to provide, in certain cases, replacement cinema projection equipment which had been destroyed by military action.

As soon as possible after cinema distribution set up its major headquarters in Paris, the section began the task of divesting itself of its functions. This process occupied several months but by the end of 1944 most of these functions had been returned to indigenous personnel, although AIS continued to provide transport where needed.

A collateral mission of the Cinema Section was the impounding of German or collaborationist films as they were uncovered.

XIII. PICTORIAL SECTION

Throughout the existence of PWD/AIS, the function of distribution of still photographs was vested in a separate section. Prior to the entry into Paris, this distribution was done on a personal basis in the various towns and cities within the consolidation area. Regular air shipments of news photographs from the various commercial agencies and from the British and American army services arrived in France and were distributed to newspaper editors on a more or less haphazard basis. Photographic window displays also were set up, as described in the section on Publications and Display.

However, after the liberation of Paris, this distributing of photographs was formalized. Following discussions with the appropriate officials of the French Ministry of Information, an agency called "Photo Presse Liberation" was designated by the Ministry as the correct channel for AIS pictures. AIS Pictorial Section supplied a daily selected file of news pictures to "Photo Presse" which, in turn, produced the required number of copies and serviced the newspapers at a fixed commercial rate to cover its expenses. AIS/PWD reserved the right to deal with other photo distribution agencies should such come into being.

As time went on, first one and then another of the regular commercial picture agencies, such as Wide World and Acme, reopened operations in Paris, and AIS/PWD, which had been servicing pictures by these agencies, ceased to do so. Later, provincial offices distributed news pictures to provincial papers.

As with the other AIS operating sections, the functions of the Pictorial Section returned eventually to the civilian agencies of OWI and MOI on a national rather than an Anglo-American basis.

The Pictorial Section, in addition to servicing the local press, serviced PWD combat propaganda teams with pictures for use in leaflets, etc.

Attached to the Pictorial Section were photographers whose task it was to photograph the war and liberated areas from the standpoint of propaganda to be used in Europe rather than, as with the American and British commercial photographers, for distribution in America and England.

XIV. STRASBOURG EPISODE

On Thanksgiving Day 1944 troops of the Armies comprising the 6th Army Group liberated the city of Strasbourg, capital of Alsace. Primary consolidation work in the information field was done by the psychological warfare combat team attached to the 7th U.S. Army. This consolidation work consisted of public address system operations in the city and surrounding countryside, bringing to the people news of the progress of the war. The city of Strasbourg was effectually cut off from the rest of France and from Paris. The radio transmitter signal of Radio Paris operated by Radio Diffusion Francaise, was inaudible in Alsace, while on the other hand certain German transmitters, particulary Radio Stuttgart, poured very strong signals into the city. To understand fully the situation that developed in Strasbourg, it must be borne in mind that the city is on the Rhine and that the Germans were on the other side of the river.

So long as the Allied armies advanced, or at least held the enemy, the morale situation in Strasbourg was no great problem. The 7th Army team continued to provide a minimum of information service for the city while waiting replacement by a French team. This was the circumstance in the isolated city of Strasbourg when the Rundstedt counter offensive began in mid-December. 7th Army combat team personnel, which had been supplying information services, was required elsewhere. The expected French team did not materialize. The German armies advanced to within a relatively few miles of the city on the north and south. With the river and the Germans to the east as well, the people of Strasbourg felt themselves to be nearly surrounded by the enemy and in a dangerous position. This was the kind of situation the enemy propagandists were able to exploit to the full; and they did so. Radio Stuttgart bombarded the jittery people of the city with tall tales, in which there was more than a gleam of truth, to the effect that it was likely the German armies would recapture Strasbourg and take reprisals against those people who had aided or cooperated with the Allied armies. The enemy propagandists' intelligence conerning details of life in the city of Strasbourg was very good and the people had the increasingly uncomfortable feeling that the enemy was behind every tree.

This situation continued until early in January, when General de Lattre de Tassigny, Commanding General of the First French Army, requested the PW Section of 6th Army Group to send personnel to Strasbourg to take steps to support civilian morale. The request for personnel was passed on to PWD/SHAEF, which immediately detailed a special Task Force composed of radio, press, news and public address people to go to Strasbourg.

The team crossed the Vosges in a blizzard, arriving late at night. The next morning the various technical experts began to investigate the situation. Previously, Radio Diffusion Française had dispatched technicians and editorial personnel to install a small radio transmitter for coverage of the Strasbourg area. The PWD radio technicians immediately turned to the task of assisting the RDF personnel in speeding up the installation of the transmitter. With this transmitter on the air, despite its relative low power, it was hoped that the people of Strasbourg would cease listening to Radio Stuttgart which perforce had been their local station.

The situation relative to the local press was almost unbelievably bad. Seven local newspapers were being published. Because of electric power shortages and because of the shoddy journalist techniques into which the Strasbourg editors had fallen during the occupation, no attempt was being made to produce these newspapers on a "hot" news basis and SHAEF communiques were reaching the public as much as forty-eight hours after release. Despite the tense local situation, the Strasbourg editors apparently had no sense of their civic responsibility to the people. They insisted that no edition of a newspaper be released to the kiosks until all copies of every paper had come off the two available presses. And because of power shortages, the time required for the run of all copies of all seven papers sometimes carried from one day to the next. This great time lag between release of the SHAEF communiques and their presentation to the public permitted Radio Stuttgart each day to reach the people of Strasbourg with an intenionally inaccurate version of the SHAEF communique before the correct version reached them. Thus, day by day, while the Rundstedt offensive actually was being contained, the people of Strasbourg continued in an increasingly jittery state, constituting a serious situation immediately in the rear of the American 7th and First French Armies.

In order to alleviate the press situation, press officers of the PWD Task Force did two things. First, they called together the editors and attempted to instill in them a sense of their responsibility in this crisis, to the end that the editors might cooperate with one another to serve the public for the time being, rather than to continue on a distinctly competitive basis. This was partially successful. Second, PWD Morse monitors undertook to provide the editors with the text of the SHAEF communiques on a "hot" basis. Where formerly the editors had allowed the communique to lie over one full day, they now kept available one column of space on page one through the morning to take the communique when it should arrive. This was a simple enought expedient but the editors themselves had not arrived at it.

Meanwhile, using the same monitoring material as was provided the newspapers, public address units, operated by personnel from the PWD Task Force, gave news bulletins in the city and the surrounding country side. Through these means the people of Strasbourg came to understand the true proportions of the military situation and when they understood that, the rise in their morale was measurable.

Within a few days of the arrival of the PWD Task Force, the transmitter of Radio Strasbourg was ready to go on the air. At this point, PWD found itself in the midst of a strange contretemps on prerogative. It must be recalled that PWD personnel had arrived in Strasbourg at the request of General de Lattre. At the same time RDF had requested that PWD radio technicians assist in the installation of the transmitter. Again it must be recalled that PWD personnel was under instructions to operate as anonymously as possible and to withdraw as soon as the situation was in hand.

In this set of circumstances and with the transmitter ready to go on the air, PWD encountered an impasse which resulted from the fact that neither the representatives of General de Lattre in Strasbourg nor the representatives of the French Ministry of Information (including RDF) in Strasbourg would retreat from the position that each controlled information activities in the city. The representatives of General de Lattre insisted that Strasbourg was still within the military zone of the First French Army. The delegate of the Ministry of Information insisted that Strasbourg, because of the nature of the city as the capital of Alsace, hat reverted for information control purposes to the gouvernment at Paris. PWD's position was that it was interested only in getting the transmitter on the air and that it could not choose between the military and civilian French leadership. The commanding officer of the PWD team stated, however, that since PWD was a military organization, its major contact must be with General de Lattre. Insofar as it was possible the PWD Task Force did not, of course, take sides in the purely French disagreement over prerogative. However, it did continue to insist that every day that passed with the available transmitter still not on the air was a victory, albeit a minor one, for the enemy. Eventually, with pressure brought to bear on high levels, the small Strasbourg transmitter went on the air running relays of Radio Paris and with certain locally initiated programs.

The people of Strasbourg began to listen to their own transmitter and slowly the effect of Radio Stuttgart was cut down. One by one PWD withdrew the members of the Task Force leaving at the end only the Morse monitors who continued to supply the newspapers and the radio station with up to the minute military news. By this time, the government at Paris and General de Lattre had reached understandings on French personnel to take over the task of continued consolidation operations in Alsace.

With the clearing of the Colmar pocket and the subsequent removal of the enemy from the vicinity of Strasbourg, PWD regarded its task as completed and withdrew the remainder of its personnel.

The foregoing is given here at this length because it appears to indicate the kind of unexpected situation which may arise in an area of consolidation wherein rear area work suddenly takes on an unwonted aspect of immediacy due to such military circumstances as the Rundstedt counteroffensive.

(Long months after the Rundstedt counteroffensive had become history—after the Wehrmacht had surrendered and the war was over—PWD again appeared on Strasbourg's horizon. But this time it was from the East. Across the river in conquered Germany, a PWD officer had come upon information that 31 church bells, stolen from villages in the Strasbourg area in 1941 by the Nazis, were stored in a warehouse near Hannover. They had been taken from 27 Catholic and Protestant churches as part of the Nazis' campaign to recover strategic metals. PWD undertook the transport of the bells across Germany to Strasbourg, and, at an impressive ceremony in the great square before the venerable cathedral, the bells were turned over to the archbishop. The date of this ceremony, the occasion of a local holiday in Strasbourg, was particularly appropriate—Assumption Day, which coincided with V-J Day.)

A PWD sound truck gives instructions to a crowd of bewildered Displaced Persons, former slave laborers, after their liberation in Darmstadt, Germany.

XV. DISPLACED PERSONS

In the final swift weeks of the Battle of Germany and in the early months of the surrender of the Wehrmacht, one of the greatest problems facing the Allies in the west was that involving United Nations Displaced Persons and liberated prisoners of war. The collecting and repatriation of these people, numbered in the millions, was an immediate task facing G-5 and G-1. PWD/SHAEF, too, had a part to play in this immense operation. As the mouthpiece for G-5 to these people, PWD embarked upon a program of instructions and entertainment, designed to inform them concerning what they were to do, and to bridge the gap between liberation and repatriation. PWD produced and disseminated certain "Voice of SHAEF" messages of instruction by radio and leaflet and circulated various periodicals.

Actually, PWD had been addressing the Displaced Persons in Germany long before they were liberated. Increasingly as the campaign against Germany had progressed, special radio programs and special leaflets addressed to foreign workers in Germany had been a part of the overall psychological warfare campaign. (A fuller understanding by G-1 and by the Displaced persons Branch of G-5 of PWD's activities in this field probably would have resulted in a smoother operation by all concerned.) It had been PWD's aim to make the various nationalities of foreign workers in Germany conscious of their joint interests and, on the other hand, to use the threat of the combined might of the foreign workers to strike fear into the German home front.

When the Allied Forces entered the first German area of large populations where many foreign workers were employed, PWD, serving to disseminate the wishes of the Supreme Commander, gave instructions to these foreign workers concerning their conduct in the face of the advancing Armies. When the Supreme Commander wished foreign workers to remain at their posts, contrary to the orders of the German High Command, PWD issued these instructions. When, later, the Supreme Commander wished the foreign workers to evacuate the cities, again contrary to the wishes of the German High Command, PWD promulgated the message. Increasingly, as the campaign neared its end, the foreign workers in Western Germany obeyed the Supreme Commander's instructions as promulgated by PWD to the letter.

By the time large numbers of foreign workers and prisoners of war had been uncovered by the Allied armies, PWD was in a position to help carry out the final phase of this aspect of the campaign. As was to be expected, the simple matter of getting home as quickly as possible was uppermost in the minds of foreign workers and liberated prisoners. The vast numbers involved constituted a serious problem in that the mere traffic of so many people moving independently would have choked the highways and other lines of transport. G-5 and G-1 plans called for collection of displaced persons and liberated prisoners in camps for orderly transport to the various countries. In order to promulgate instructions to this end, PWD reoriented many of its radio broadcasts, particulary at Radio Luxembourg. A daily four-language airborne newspaper was inaugurated. It was called "SHAEF" and was printed at first in English, German, French, and Polish. Later, Russian replaced the German. This newspaper was produced in London and was flown each night by the special leaflet squadron of the 8th Air Force. It reached a maximum circulation of 2,000,000 daily before it was replaced by a weekly newspaper of larger format. SHAEF

6 The Psychological Warfare

was dropped both in leaflet bombs and later in bundles by parachute on pin-pointed targets near displaced persons camps. When most of the displaced persons had been collected in camps and repatriation had begun—when, in fact, the displaced persons had nothing to do but wait—the tiny total of news contained in the original SHAEF newspaper was not sufficient to satisfy their needs. Thus, the second SHAEF newspaper was eight pages instead of four, giving each language two sides for news and information. This newspaper was produced once a week in Russian, Polish, French, and Italian. In order to continue dissemination of this for as long as necessary special dispensation was granted for the services of the special leaflet squadron beyond the original termination date of June 20.

PWD undertook to sponsor circulation of several other kinds of newspapers to displaced persons. Among these were:

(a) A Yugoslav weekly newspaper, prepared under the auspices of the Yugoslav government through the Yugoslav representative in the SHAEF European Contact Section. This paper was produced in Paris and had originally been distributed on a haphazard basis by Yugoslaw liaison officers.

(b) Two Czech weekly newspapers. These newspapers were published in London under the control of the Chief of the PID Czech Desk. They were bundled for shipment (5,000 copies each) with the SHAEF newspaper and dispatched to 12th Army Group for distribution. Later, arrangements were made with the Czech Mission for distribution on a basis similar to that of the Yugoslav newspaper.

(c) A French weekly newspaper. This was published by a French team attached to 12th Army Group at Frankfurt. The paper, called "RETOUR," had a circulation of 200,000.

Beyond this, PWD arranged with the civilian agencies for publication of a booklet called "Since 1939," an objective word-and-picture story of the war. This booklet, which had been circulated elsewhere in various languages, was brought up to date to include the German surrender and was translated into Russian and Polish.

Weekly editions of "Communique Graphique," a news-in-pictures bulletin board poster was issued in French, Russian, Polish, Italian, Yugoslav, Czech and Dutch.

The civilian agencies, OWI and MOI, made available to PWD/SHAEF large quantities of various kinds of booklets and brochures which were left over from previous operations. Every effort was made to prevent the displaced persons camps from being regarded as a trash basket for unused printed material. However, the need was great and appropriate material was put to this final use.

With the German surrender, Radio Luxembourg for a period devoted the majority of its air time to displaced persons broadcasts and, beyond this, BBC, ABSIE and The Voice of America furnished special programs for relay by Radio Luxembourg and by the German Network. Schedules were published regularly in "SHAEF." PWD undertook to assist camp supervisors in finding and installing radio receivers in the camps.

Beginning the second week in June 1945, weekly newsreels with Russian, French, and Polish sound tracks were made available for showing in displaced persons camps. Twenty-five American documentary short films with French, Czech, and Polish subtitles and forty British documentaries in Czech and Polish were provided.

About the middle of June, a mobile motion picture projection unit was put to use in displaced persons camps in each of the Army Group areas. These units were complete with a full stock of various kinds of films in several languages, but were woefully inadquate for the size of the task.

The displaced persons problem in general was considered originally as a short-term one. In the early weeks following the German surrender, the repatriation of Western Europe went forward at a high rate of speed. Eastern Europeans required longer to be moved, but by mid-June had reached a rate of 30,000 a day for the Russians. The polish repatriation problem was by all odds the most difficult and became an extremely long-term problem. It can be seen that the PWD task involving instructions and entertainment for displaced persons was one which perforce had to get underway quickly and reach its maximum tempo almost at once. It appears that it may be stated safely that PWD's contribution was responsible for some small part of the success of the entire effort in repatriation of displaced persons and prisoners of war.

In the field of Displaced Persons, as in so many others, PWD often found itself in strange by-ways. PWD officers came upon the poignant cases of Polish children, some born in Germany, others brought to Germany at an early age with their slave-laborer parents. These children had never seen their native language in print and had never learned to read. The German neglect of them had been absolute.

In the Displaced Persons camps in Germany, the need for primary education for these unhappy children became manifest. Polish adults attempted to provide this, but there were no textbooks in Polish. PWD officers were shocked to find that the Polish page of the weekly "SHAEF" air newspaper was being used as a primer to teach the children their A-B-C's.

In order to fulfill a basic need as simply as possible, PWD inaugurated a weekly newspaper in Polish designed specifically for children in Displaced Persons camps. Through this paper, some 15,000 Polish children learned the rudiments of their native language.

(One incident may illustrate the success of PWD's campaign directed toward foreign workers in Germany during the final hectic weeks of the war. A British woman correspondent was covering the entry of American troops into a suburb of Frankfurt. She saw groups of foreign workers emerging from the woods outside the town, and spoke to them. They were jubilant.

"We obeyed his orders," they said.

"Whose orders?" she wanted to know.

With that they pulled from their pockets the PWD leaflets giving General Eisenhower's precise instructions on how to conduct themselves in the face of the Allied advance. In this particular case, they had been instructed to leave the factories and hide in the woods. And they had done it to the letter.)

XVI. CONTROL OF GERMAN INFORMATION SERVICES

Up to this point practically all of the discussion in this history was concerned with psychological warfare activities against the enemy and information services for liberated Allied countries. As this is written, much has been planned but relatively little has been done on the positive side in the third of PWD's major missions, namely, control of German information services.

Attached to this history as an appendix is the PWD Manual for Control of German Information Services. It gives, medium by medium, the plan under which PWD undertook its task in occupied Germany.

The structure of the Psychological Warfare Division organization changed somewhat with the end of the war in Europe. The Leaflet Section was abolished. The Film Section which had, in effect, not existed at all after AIS returned the distribution of films in liberated countries to the civilian agencies, was revived in a much larger way with added responsibilities. This Section became known as Films-Theater-Music Control Section. The Liberated Areas and Special Liaison office, which had been set up during the last days of AIS was abolished. The Directives Section and the Plans and Organization Section became a single section known as Plans and Directives. The Displaced Persons and Prisoners of War Section was formalized.

Colonel William S. Paley was named Deputy Chief of PWD in charge of Operations. An assistant to the Chief of PWD in charge of control of German information services was appointed. He was Mr. C. D. Jackson, who had been Chief of AIS and civilian deputy to General McClure from the inception of PWD. What remained of the older system of four civilian deputies, each primarily responsible for one or several of the operating sections, thus disappeared.

The field force for German information control took the form of District Information Service Control Commands. In what became the American Zone, units operated in Munich and Wiesbaden. In what became the British Zone (but still during the SHAEF period) units operated in Hamburg, Hannover and Oelde. These units had operating sections, namely Intelligence, Publications, Press, Radio, and Films-Theater-Music.

PWD/SHAEF (Main) moved its headquarters from Paris to Bad Homburg, Germany, June 15—16, 1945. However, long before this move was made, PWD units had been engaged on certain aspects of the task of control of German information services and published its handbook paralleling similar Military Government publications. PWD separated the work in Germany into three phases. The first phase went into effect in each German locality directly it was captured. This called for the immediate shut-down of German information services. The second phase provided for the institution of *Allied* information services, utilizing German newspaper and publishing plants, radio transmitters, etc. The writing and editing was done by Allied personnel. The third phase envisaged a gradual transition from *Allied* information services to *German-managed* services working under Allied supervision. Necessarily, this third phase could begin only after detailed reconnaissance and examination of prospetive German operators had been made. A lengthy and detailed guinea pig experiment had been conducted in the field of the press which was presumed to provide an example of the kind of problems to be encountered in nearly every media. This took place in Aachen and a full account of the experience gained there will be given later.

As noted above, the first, or shutdown phase, of PWD operations in Germany went into effect piecemeal as the country was occupied. The second phase began with the reopening of 100-kilowatt radio transmitters in Munich, Stuttgart and Hamburg. These transmitters gave most of their broadcast time to relays from the key PWD station at Luxembourg. A small mobile transmitter was installed at Frankfurt to replace the transmitter which was completely destroyed by the enemy. During this second phase, overt Allied Army newspapers were published for the local population of Germany. Ten plants were being used, covering major population centers in the Anglo-American Zone such as Essen, Cologne, Frankfurt, Kassel and Munich. In this second phase of the program, the emphasis, was on publicizing Military Government rules and regulations, countering rumors by announcements, and supplying a selected news service. The part of this news service dealing with world news (everything, in fact, except local news) was produced in the United Kingdom by the Allied Press Service. The A.P.S. news file was a synthesis of material available from the usual agency an official sources. It was beamed daily to the continent by radio and was the major source of world news for all newspapers published in the Anglo-American Zones.

The immediate objectives of the Allied Information Services were: (1) to maintain and deepen the mood of passive acquiescence and acceptance of orders to the German people and so to facilitate the completion of the occupation of Germany; (2) to undertake special campaigns required by Military Government; and (3) to take the first steps toward arousing a sense of collective responsibility for Germany's crimes and to provide the facts designed to expose the vital consequences of Nazi and militarist leadership and German acquiescence in them. PWD did not indulge in argumentative propaganda but confined itself to unemotional reporting and instructions.

Preparation for the third and final phase of PWD's work—the gradual turning over of information services to Germans who would function under Allied supervision—was necessarily long. Reconnaissance missions to discover Germans who might be trusted to publish newspapers or books, to produce films, etc., were instructed to leave no stone unturned in probing the background, political tone and character of the men whom they would recommend. Investigators were instructed not only to test candidates for past affiliation with the Nazi party, but further, to explore the backgrounds of professed non-Nazis for traces of militarist or German nationalist beliefs.

(NOTE.—Chapter XXII of this account goes into greater detail in discussing the German Information Control function. In small part it is a repetition of the above, but carries the account to the end of September 1945. It discusses the work of the Information Control Division, United States Forces, European Theater, which was the successor of PWD SHAEF in the American Zone of Occupation.)

XVII. THE NEWSPAPER AT AACHEN

The battered city of Aachen fell to Allied troops in mid-October 1944. This was the first community of appreciable size in Germany to fall into Allied hands, and thus, despite the wreckage, it offered opportunity for laboratory experimentation in information control activities.

The Psychological Warfare Branch, 12th Army Group, circulated in Aachen its weekly newspaper called "DIE MITTEILUNGEN," but no newspaper was published in Aachen itself for some two and one-half months after the city fell.

Meanwhile the Press Section of PWD/SHAEF began negotiations with 12th Army Group for concurrence in its plan to conduct the Aachen press experiment. During the weeks following the fall of the city a small team of PWD/SHAEF press personnel, including editor, circulation-liaison officer, Morse monitors, etc., arrived in the city. The plant of "Politisches Tageblatt" was requisitioned and the persons occupying the building, including the controlling director of the paper, were moved out.

The PWD team recognized that its problem was not so much one of providing Aachen with a newspaper as of finding the right man for eventual licensing as publisher. In all of the early planning for PWD operations in Germany, it had been manifest that technical ability in the various fields would be far easier to find than political purity. The question to be answered was this: Would it be better to compromise on technical ability or on the political background of the eventual licensee? In theory, PWD was certain of the answer. There must be no compromise in the matter of Nazi or militarist associations of the licensee. In practice, however, PWD personnel would be forced to make certain compromises on technical ability and the Aachen experiment was to show just to what extent this would be necessary.

Early in January, when the PWD team was ready to select the prospective licensee as publisher, the available candidates in Aachen were few. One was the controlling director of the "Politisches Tageblatt" which had continued publication until the city's fall. This man was engaged in January in printing proclamations, etc. for Military Government. Investigation showed that he had been an S.A. man in 1934 and had been a member of the Nazi party in good standing since 1937. A second candidate also had an unsavory political background.

The third candidate, Heinrich Hollands, was a veteran Social Democrat and had done no newspaper work between 1933 and late 1944. Except for the eleven-year-gap, Hollands had spent his life in newspapers and printing. He had owned his own printing works at one time and had been active in management of Social Democrat newspapers. Comprehensive investigation convinced the PWD team that Hollands had remained out of newspaper work since 1933 because of his sincere anti-Nazi convictions. During this inactive period he had supported his family on a monthly pension of 94 marks. When the PWD team came to Aachen, Hollands was serving as technical manager of the Politisches Tageblatt plant on the Military Government work. Although Hollands appeared to have a clean political record, and although his technical knowledge of the printing side of newspaper was unassailable, he knew little about the editorial side. Weighing the pros and cons of the available candidates, the PWD team determined to give Hollands an opportunity to work toward an eventual license. This meant, however, that the PWD team would be forced to give Hollands much advice and guidance before he would be qualified to publish the paper alone.

Meanwhile, the damaged plant had been repaired and the first copy of the newspaper in Aachen, called the "AACHENER NACHRICHTEN," was published on January 24, 1945. The paper was a weekly. Acceptable personnel to fill the key positions on the paper under Hollands was assembled gradually. At first, the editorial side was handled entirely by the PWD team, using the Allied Press Service news file and local Military Government and other items. Certain sharp changes in the style of German journalism were introduced, notably the factual objective reporting of news, separation of news and comment, and the speeding up of the tone of headlines. Hollands and the local personnel under him appeared to accept these changes with good grace.

Population surveys showed that the form of the new paper met with approval. The circulation, which began at 12,000 per week, rose steadily to 52,000.

In publishing the Aachen paper, the PWD team hewed closely to the line of SHAEF directives. The circulation of the paper outside Aachen itself was accomplished by jeep through Military Government Detachments and special arrangements with burgomeisters.

In its early period the paper was of extreme value to the occupying forces, particularly when the fighting front still was very near the city and community life was completely dead; the people were living in scattered groups all over the town, wherever there was a whole roof. And, naturally, Aachen and the surrounding communities were alive with fantastic rumors. The people required something to give them a sense of continuity in daily life, and the AACHENER NACHRICHTEN did this through its week by week Military Government instructions and world news.

It is not necessary here to dwell on the manifold mechanical problems that beset the PWD team. Mostly these involved electric power for the presses and linotype machines. Week by week the appearance of the paper on the streets was a matter of question up to the last moment since one never knew when, or if, there would be power.

The PWD directive which called for eventual licensing of newspapers implied that the team working in Aachen must build up the self-confidence and self-sufficiency of the Germans who had been tentatively selected for licensing. When Hollands' ideas concerning a particular issue of the paper did not measure up to the standards set by the PWD team, the team advised changes but did not order them. In this way a certain degree of educating was done looking toward the time when the Germans would have to stand largely on their own feet. By mid-June the German group in Aachen was able to edit, manage, and distribute the paper on its own.

The main proposals made by Hollands concerning the business management of the paper were:

(1) There should be no stockholders but the net profits of the paper should be divided thus: 25% to go into a blocked bank account to take care of later possible claims until a sum equalling the total value of the property (191,000 marks) is in the account; 10% to the chief editor; 5% to the editor; 5% to the business manager; 5% to the office manager, 5% to the chief printer; 15% to a fund for sickness, etc.

(2) In June 1945 the paper had assets of 50,000 marks, 42,000 of which was cash in bank. Hollands proposed that 25,000 marks of this should remain in the blocked account, the remainder to be freed as operating capital.

Late in June 1945, Hollands was granted a conditional license to publish the paper in Aachen, the first such license in Germany.

XVIII. COMMUNICATIONS

In the early days, there was no Communications Section for the Publicity and Psychological Warfare Division.

At this time, problems affecting communications, in very minor degree, were handled by the Liaison Sub-Section of Signal Division SHAEF, whose job it was to coordinate the requirements of all agencies not directly operational. The first Signal Instruction issued stated that "P and P.W. as a Staff Division were fully entitled to the use of operational channels..." This, for the time being took care of communication requirements.

With the growth of PWD and the formation of G-6 as a General Staff Division, the new T O. included a Communications Branch which was to take care of Publicity (Press) and Psychological Warfare (PW). Although the two parts of G-6 worked in separate buildings and mainly on separate plans, the single Communications Section took care of both projects. Early in 1944, a three-officer section was transferred from Signal Division, SHAEF, and early April 1944, problems for both 'P' and 'PW' were discussed with the various sections and a plan was prepared for pre-D-Day, for D-Day and for D plus 30, D plus 60, D plus 90.

During this planning stage many meetings were held with Signal Division SHAEF through its Liaison Sub-Section, with the General Post office, the BBC, the War Office and with representatives of the OWI, who were largely connected with the Psychological Warfare aspect of the plans.

The first and original plan for PW communication activities, mainly connected with broadcasting, was drawn up by the OWI and submitted to the Chief of the Branch of P & PW, and this was passed to Liaison Sub-Section of the Signal Division for comment. Subsequently the plan was redrafted by Communications Branch and the ideas set out were incorporated in the larger plan.

By mid April 1944 the finished plan for the initial requirements of P & PW had been completed and was put into operation.

On the Psychological Warfare side, Inveresk House had been selected as Headquarters and the necessary lines and equipment were ordered through Signal Division and thence via the War Office to the GPO to guarantee news services with incoming material, teleprinter channels to commercial companies to cover contact with the world outside Europe—including the United States—and, finally, arrangements were made to take over GPO radio transmitters for transmitting by speech and morse the latest news items for liberated countries and for news and guidance to persons still in occupied zones.

The bulk of this work was completed by 31st May, and the studio built on the third floor of Inveresk House. The auomatic senders for the Morse files were completed and tested by June 4, 1944.

To take care of operational, administrative, and executive traffic, sinse PW was not located with or near SHAEF Headquarters, two circuits were provided from Inveresk House—one to the War Office terminal, which at this time was under SHAEF in Goodge Street, and one to the U.S. Headquarters ETOUSA in Duke Street.

Additional private wires were installed on the Inveresk House switchboard to all main military boards and special agencies such as MOI, PID and BBC.

On D-Day, all PW services as planned were functioning and traffic was steadily building up. News material from all the main services was flowing into the News Section, and schedules were set up for transmitting special news services to France. This included Voice casts at dictation speed.

A TO. for a PWD Communications Section of two officers and three enlisted men was set up within PWD.

On D-Day there were twenty-eight teleprinter circuits, eight news ticker services, three Morse circuits and the Voice Casting service working for PWD with an average of 21,000 words daily (6,000 in speech, and 15,000 in Morse). As operations on the continent proceeded and more countries were liberated, it became necessary to increase the news services to include other languages and more material was needed.

On May 24, 1944 a teleprinter circuit was put into ABSIE, to furnish a special file for broadcasting, and a drop line to the OWI Photo Section and the American Embassy. On August 18, 1944 the Voice Cast was stopped and its transmitter changed over to a Morse service. As this time, the service was being used in the Mediterranean theater as well as on the Continent.

In September, plans were made for a "crash location" so that in the event of bomb damage to Inveresk House a limited service could be carried on from the new headquarters, 49 Carlos Place, or from the basement of Inveresk House.

Additional services were required for the Northwestern European Theater and in August negotiations were carried out with the War Office for the loan of a British military low power transmitter. This was installed and operated by the GPO radio station at Leafield and on August 17 this set came into service as daytime transmitter for French, Belgian, and Dutch news services.

Operational traffic was now reaching a high level and there were long delays on messages. Consequently plans were made for a radio net for PWD/SHAEF. Permission was obtained from Signal Division to install and operate a radio station at Inveresk House, and arrangements were made with the 4th and 5th MRB companies to provide the equipment and personnel for London and the new headquarters at Paris. Plans for the future included the station at Radio Luxembourg; and on September 9, 1944 this channel came into use.

In early October 1944 the requirement for news on the continent had reached such proportions that all services were extended to 24 hours daily and three GPO and one military station were working for PWD. A Signal Corps radio station, working back to the United States, was handling PWD material for New York and Washington through the Overseas Room at ETOUSA (later U.K. Base).

In November the station at Radio Luxembourg joined the PWD net, giving direct contact between London, Paris, and Luxembourg for operational traffic.

In December the first intimation was receeived of the possible use of Hellschreiber, and plans made accordingly. The question of obtaining a 50 KW transmitter from the OWI was finally dropped and negotiations commenced with the Air Ministry for the loan of an AVT 22B station of 5 KW.

Also during this period the Communications Section assisted the newly formed Information Control Service Section on details of equipment for press and monitoring teams to be set up in Germany.

In January and February 1945, the Danish and Norwegian operations came into the picture and frequencies were cleared for the Norwegian Force, and for the Danish and Norwegian news files. On February 11, the Air Ministry set (AVT 22B) was sent to Leafield, where the GPO erected it and prepared it for use.

In March 1945, PWB/AFHQ moved northwards and this neccessitated the changing of frequencies for the Mediterranean service, and a plan was discussed with a view to bringing PWB/AFHQ into the PWD operational net. Tests were carried out with PWB frequencies but permission could not be obtained for their use from the U.K.

By early April operational traffic was flowing in and out of Inveresk House by PWD radio to Paris and Luxembourg, by teleprinter via Duke Street and Goodge Street to all Army Groups, Armies and other units connected with PW activities, to the United States via Signal Corps channels, and to neutral countries via commercial channels.

Five radio transmitters were now handling news services in English, French, Dutch, Flemish, and German for the Mediterranean and European Theater and a special teleprinter service was feeding material into the printing production headquarters outside London for the preparation of leaflets and the special newspaper "SHAEF."

The following shows the average daily wordage passing through PWD during this period:

(a) Administrative and operational traffic: 4500 words per day, by radio and teletype.

(b) News Services:

In English to Mediterranean and dualled later to Norway and Denmark—19,000 words per day.

In English, French, and Duch, etc., to Western Europe—26,000 words per day.

In German to Western Germany—9,000 words per day.

In English to United States via U.S. Signal Corps channels—25,000 words per day. Via Western Union—3,000 words per day.

(c) Guidance, Instructions and Analysis To Paris by teletype—1,000 words per day.

Propaganda analysis via high speed Morse—3,500 words per day. (PWD Radio net.)

Propanal to Radio Luxembourg by teletype—3,500 words per day.

(d) Special news for „SHAEF" by teletype—1,800 words per day.

Cross channel trunk and outside telephone calls from Inveresk House at this period were averaging 850 calls per day. (This does not include internal calls which at peak periods were 350 an hour.)

Courier services, including local DRLS, and ADLS services handled an average of 750 packages per day.

On May 14 the station at Leafield came into operation with Danish and Norwegian news file and additional operational traffic was handled via the War Office circuit.

Russian-controlled radio stations were now back on the air but could not be heard in the U.K. so some arrangements were made on behalf of the BBC to get back reports from the British and U.S. Army Groups. These proved satisfactory and were used by the BBC in their monitoring service.

The end of May 1945 saw the beginning of the reserve operation and with the taking over by the French and Belgian agencies of their own news services, the PWD news service to these two countries was closed down.

Early in June 1945 the Hellschreiber situation became more prominent, and equipment was collected by Army Groups. In the U.S. Zone in particular large quantities were found and quickly put into serviceable condition.

Transmission tests of Hellschreiber were commenced by PID for the Joint Allied Press Service (APS) and mid June saw the commencement of a Hellschreiber service from 1200 hours to midnight daily, with a dual transmission of the German news file still going out on Morse on the German frequencies since all points in Germany were not yet equipped with Hellschreiber receivers.

Also in early June, PWD (Main) moved to Bad Homburg and the operational circuit was moved in two steps so that there was no interruption in Communications. The standby SCR 399 was used as intermediate station and later (June 16) when the 1 KW had been installed at the news headquarters, the SCR 399 was prepared as a mobile unit ready to move into Berlin.

Plans were prepared on June 5 for the eventual closing down of PWD/SHAEF services and for the transfer of activities to Information Control Division, United States Forces European Theater. On May 30, the ABSIE service had been closed and on June 30 the Mediterranean and continental news files were stopped.

By the first of July, two GPO transmitters had been returned and several lines and terminal equipment returned to the War Office. On July 6 the final letter to the War Office disposed of all lines, equipment and transmitters, with the exception of two operational teleprinters and the two transmitters and automatic equipment still in use on the German news file. These were to remain in use until the termination of CALA.

On the closing down of SHAEF, the operational net at Inveresk House became a part of the Information Control Division network, and the operational and news services teletype channels were taken over by the Office of War Information.

XIX. FINANCIAL AND BUSINESS MANAGEMENT

In the beginning, PWD had no funds of its own. From its inception, and until May 15, 1944, all materials in the United Kingdom were supplied by the Army and by the civilian contributing agencies. On May 15th, the Fiscal Section was set up, and thenceforth PWD functioned from a basic fund and not on piecemeal handouts.

Funds—that is, money on hand or available, rather than supplies themselves—were contributed on a 50—50 basis by the British and American governments. The American contribution was split between the Office of War Information and the Office of Strategic Services; the British, among the Ministry of Information, Political Intelligence Department of the Foreign Office and the BBC for their agreed shares.

The first fund was $35,000, of which OSS contributed $25,000 und OWI $10,000 The MOI paid in no actual money, but undertook to meet half of all bills.

Agent cashiers representing the PWD/SHAEF Fiscal Section were attached to Army Group and Army psychological warfare teams, and to AIS. They received funds from the PWD Fiscal Section and rendered their accountings back to that section. All expenditures of PWD funds made by these teams required the certifying endorsement of the team chiefs.

The total sum expended by PWD from May 15th until the windup of its operations was approximately $150,000. It must be emphasized that this expenditure from the so-called PWD Operational Field Fund did not take into account the salaries of PWD American and British civilians nor did it reflect the cost of the vast quantity of supplies and equipment obtained through Army requisition, nor the cost of production of government publications and films. took in $2,061,188.37 broken down this way:

In Liberated countries, PWD took in large sums from sale of publications (see Chapter X) and from exhibition of British and American government-produced films (see Chapter XII). Beyond this, PWD received moneys for exhibition of British and American commercial films, but there were paid back to MOI and OWI for direct transmittal to the owning companies.

From sale of *government-produced* publications in Liberated countries, PWD took in $ 2,061,188.37 broken down this way:

France	$1,242,488.68
Belgium	425,581.33
Luxembourg	14,647.66
Denmark	42,930.03
Holland	330,540.67
Norway	5,000.00
	$2,061,188.37

From exhibition of *government-produced* films in Liberated countries, PWD took in a total of about $400,000.

The basic restrictive tenet of PWD's fiscal management operation was that no supplies were to be purchased on the open market until every possible Army source had been exhausted.

ICD's fiscal management differed from PWD's in one main particular. ICD obtained approval from the Chief of Staff, U.S. Forces European Theater to utilize funds received from sale of government publications and exhibition of government-produced films to pay expenses of reimbursable enterprises. This constituted, then, a sort of pump-priming fund and was an unusual feature of government fiscal procedure. It proved extremely valuable, because although ICD was often able to place the cost of varicus enterprises at the doorsteps of the appropriate local burgomeisters, it was sometimes necessary to make an original investment in a newspaper, for instance, in order to get it started quickly.

ICD operated in requisitioned newspaper plants, using requisitioned newsprint stocks, and, because of the nature of the military occupation, avoided normal operating costs in other ways. On this basis, as of the end of September, 1945, "profits" (if they can legitimately be called such) of some $250,000 were held by ICD.

In the absence in Germany of commercial film distributors, holders of United States book copyrights, etc., ICD undertook the business management of these enterprises. However, ICD planned to divest itself of these responsibilities as soon as possible, when American commercial interests should be in position to negotiate directly with Germans.

XX. SUPPLY AND TRANSPORT

It was less than two months before D-Day, on April 28, 1944, that the Supply and Transport Section was organized as an integral part of PWD/SHAEF. The section's responsibilities lay in the procurement, warehousing, and shipping of the manifold varieties of supplies contemplated for use in psychological warfare. Soon after D-Day the section shouldered the burden of supplying field operations not only in respect of AIS, which was a direct off-shoot of PWD/SHAEF, but the psychological warfare teams with Army Groups and Armies as well.

Insufficiency of personnel and transport inhibited the operation throughout, as did the fact that PWD had already been granted a low priority by S-4, Headquarters Command. Many suplies of a specialized and technical nature were procured through PWD's civilian contributing agencies and a Joint Procurement Committee comprising PWD, OWI, OSS, PID and MOI was established in London.

In order to carry out its various tasks, the section established and maintained the following units within itself:

(a) An Administrative Unit responsible for the overall planning and operation of the section.

(b) A Requisitions and Inventories Unit responsible for procurement of all supplies and maintenance of adequate records covering issuance of materiel.

(c) A Shipping Unit responsible for the movemont by air, sea, rail and truck of all psychological warfare supplies from issuing depots to units in the field.

(d) A Warehousing Unit responsible for storage of all bulk supplies and for the proper maintenance of warehouse levels of materiel.

(e) A Transportation Unit responsible for the operation and maintenance of all vehicles assigned or attached to the Division whether at Headquarters or with Division units in the field.

(f) A Port Detachment Unit originally established at Cherbourg and subsequently moved to Rouen to process incoming shipments of psychological warfare supplies from the United Kingdom to the continent. *A total of in excess of 8,000 tons of psychological warfare materiel was processed in transit through these detachments.*

(g) A Joint Procurement Board Unit which was charged with the responsibility of obtaining supplies of a highly technical and specialized nature through civilian agencies.

(h) A Liaison Unit with the civilian agencies through which all requisitons for specialized equipment were processed.

Among supplies procured by this section in behalf of the Psychological Warfare operation were all types of office equipment, including typewriters, over 750 of which were in simultaneous operation; complete radio sets and radio parts and equipment, most of which were jointly supplied through the civilian agencies; all types of public address systems utilized by both the consolidation and combat teams in the field; press monitoring equipment required for the establishment of news outposts in the field; immense stocks of all types of paper for maintenance of the leaflet program in combat operations and newspaper and publications program in consolidation operations; all types of film, including moving pictures and display photographs; all types of photographic equipment and the procurement of highly specialized technical equipment such as radio transmitters and radio towers.

XXI. THE PROBLEM OF NEWSPRINT

It is probable that PWD faced no single problem quite as complex and as difficult of solution as that involving the supply of newsprint for its own operations and those in which it was interested secondarily.

Like so many other PWD problems there was a background of experience to be gleaned from the work of PWB in AFHQ. The background of the problem was similar in AFHQ and in SHAEF.

Newsprint is heavy and bulky and its shipment is difficult under war time conditions. Beyond this, newsprint was in increasingly short supply as the war went on. Finally, the various users of newsprint within SHAEF were varied and a delicately balanced scale of priorities was required for allocation of the stuff of which printed matter is made.

A year after the beginning of the "TORCH" operation PWB/AFHQ initiated establishment of an Allied Publications Board for allocation of newsprint in the liberated areas of Italy. The newsprint coordinator of PWB served as chairman of this Board on which were represented other aspects of the AFHQ hierarchy which used newsprint. In general, in Italy and in Northwestern Europe there were three primary large users of newsprint. These were:

(1) The "STARS & STRIPES" and other American or British troop newspapers and publications.

(2) Newspapers and other publications published by liberated governments or individuals in liberated areas.

(3) Psychological Warfare—newspapers, publications, leaflets, etc.

Before the establishment of the Allied Publications Board in AFHQ these three prime users of newsprint were in direct competition with one another at all times, with the result that to a large extent the available supply of newsprint was neither allocated nor used on an equitable or efficient basis. In certain cases there was hoarding of newsprint stocks by one or another of the competing groups and other similar dodges to lay up stocks against what was always imminent danger of complete drought. PWB, as the instigator of the Allied Publications Board, undertook the task of supplying all three users on a continuing basis. Careful estimates of the overall monthly newsprint needs were made and arrangements concluded for regular shipment of the required amounts.

Against this background PWD/SHAEF entered upon solution of the newsprint problem in its Theater. However, mere background knowledge did not solve the problem. The newsprint requirements in Northwestern Europe were infinitely greater than those in AFHQ. Because of the greater importance of the theater and the larger numbers of Allied troops involved, the "STARS & STRIPES" newsprint requirements were well-nigh astronomical. Newspapers in the liberated countries of Northwestern Europe were not under the complete jurisdiction of PWD and consequently PWD could not control from month to month the establishment of new papers which would eat unexpectedly into the available newsprint stocks. Supply of newsprint for newspapers in these liberated countries had to be negotiated through the liberated governments which meant far more negotiation and a much more involved chain of liaison. PWD's use of leaflets, booklets, brochures, etc. were vastly greater in scope than those of PWB/AFHQ. Thus, although the principle of supplying newsprint for all uses on the continent was the same in SHAEF as it had been in the mature days of AFHQ, the working out of the problem was by no means simple.

By the time of the German surrender a fourth aspect was added to the problem. This was the publication on an increasingly large scale of newspapers in Germany. This was done either under Army Group or PWD/SHAEF supervision and the delicate problem of priorities again arose, based on the question of whether, in the event of unexpected shortage, the PWD program involving newspapers in Germany should suffer or one of the other major users of newsprint.

To be sure, with the end of the war, certain stocks of newsprint were uncovered in Germany. By the same token, however, requisitioning of German coal for other purposes outside Germany brought the German newsprint manufacturing industry almost to a standstill. Thus, newsprint used in Germany in the early months after complete occupation was taken from rapidly diminishing stocks on hand with little prospect of immediate replenishment. And in view of newsprint shortages in Britain and America, to say nothing of far greater shortages in the liberated countries, it was obvious that newsprint would not be shipped *into* Germany in the immediate future.

As this is written, the problem of newsprint supply for PWD's program in Germany is still too far from being sorted out to permit much constructive discussion.

However, in order to demonstrate the complexity of the entire newsprint problem, the burden of which fell upon PWD, some notes taken from a report dated 18 March 1945 on the French newsprint situation may be helpful.

The French newsprint program, which went into effect in September 1944, soon after the liberation of Paris, called for monthly consumption of 5,200 tons of paper. This program had been concurred in by PWD/SHAEF and the SHAEF Mission to France. By mid-January of 1945 a shortage of available newsprint had perforce curtailed the size of French newspapers and the French requirement per month was reduced to between 2,500 and 3,000 tons. At the beginning of 1945 there was on hand at French newsprint mills sufficient wood for pulping to manufacture 9,600 tons of newsprint. This was to be produced by the end of March and would thus exhaust all pulp on hand.

It was estimated that deliveries of newsprint from Switzerland for the first three months of 1945 would total approximately 2,400 tons. It was hoped that this total might be increased by 1,000 tons through the supply by the French to the Swiss of a special shipment of coal. At the same time there appeared reason to hope that a further 500 to 800 tons of paper per month might be forthcoming from Switzerland.

Meanwhile a French governmental mission had arranged with the American government for procurement of 10,000 tons of newsprint and 3,000 tons of pulping. This was to augment French requirements up to July 1, 1945. At the same time there were found in the harbor at Antwerp after its liberation, 2,000 tons of newsprint which had been en route to France from Sweden. This newsprint was used by the Belgians. France demanded repayment and Belgium agreed to comply. At this time there were available 400 tons of Swiss manufactured newsprint which had been destined for Belgium and arrangements were made to ship this to France instead. Further contribution toward completion of the French newsprint program came when the British government directed the British Newsprint Supply Company (the newsprint holding company for the British press) to release 2,000 tons of newsprint to France.

Finally, in February, SHAEF delivered to the French government just under

2,000 tons of newsprint through COM Z. This supply program was based on SHAEF plans for the liberated areas of Northwestern Europe. Allocations were made on a quarterly basis dating from D-Day. Thus, June, July, and August 1944 constituted the first quarter. As indicated by the February deliveries it was regarded as encouraging that this supply program was actually working. Allocations for shipping space for this program were dependent upon the changing and unpredictable military combat priorities.

All of the foregoing has been noted here in order to indicate the complexity of the newsprint supply problem. As time went on, demands for newsprint increased but shiping tonnage remained static. The roblem grew larger rather than smaller. And with the end of the war in Europe, the pressures to relieve newsprint shortages in Britain and America made the problem even more involved.

Generally speaking, PWD managed always to make ends meet but this was based on an absolute minimum use of newsprint for newspapers in the liberated countries and in Germany. Newspapers of luxurious size never were an aim and certainly never were a fact.

XXII. STATUS OF CONTROL OF GERMAN SERVICES IN THE AMERICAN ZONE AS OF THE END OF SEPTEMBER, 1945

As of midnight, July 13, 1945—the date of the dissolution of SHAEF—most of the work accomplished by PWD in its final task of controlling German information services had been in the preliminary and planning aspects of the mission.

As has been shown, the policy of procedure under which PWD began its task, and under which ICD/USFET and ICS/USGCC continued it, was divided into three phases.

In the first phase, all media of public expression in Germany were to be shut down. This was done piecemeal as the Allied armies advanced across Germany.

The second phase called for overt operation of certain selected instruments of public information—radio transmitters, newspapers, etc.—*by the Allied Forces.* Where possible and necessary, German personnel was to assist Allied personnel, but only in technical or similar capacities. No attempt was to be made to cause the German poeple to believe other than that the instruments were under complete control of the Allied forces. Clearly-labelled overt weekly newpspapers were to be published by PW teams of Army Groups to fulfill the immediate need for information in Germany, transmitting Military Government instructions, etc. The German radio was to be operated on the same basis as an instrument of Military Government.

The third phase of the information control plan envisaged the gradual turning over of the various instruments by means of licenses to carefully selected anti-Nazi, democratic-minded Germans. This third phase itself was divided into three stages. In the first stage, PWD retained the right of pre-publication scrutiny of all material published by a licensee. (Later, a directive eliminated this pre-publication scrutiny, save for military security.) In the second, the licensee would be subjected only to post-publication scrutiny of his output. The third stage, called for ultimate removal of all such restrictions and controls.

In actual operation, the licensing procedure was a slow and laborious one. Sometimes months were required before an individual or a group had been completely vetted. However, PWD and its successor in the American Zone after the dissolution of SHAEF believed that without a firm foundation of integrity no ultimate success could be obtained for the control program's philosophy that German information media must be turned over to Germans as quickly as was safely possible. It was PWD's belief that any ultimate re-education of Germans along anti-Nazi and anti-militarist lines must be accomplished by Germans speaking to Germans of their own clear conviction that democracy must replace the habit of dictatorship.

By the end of PWD/SHAEF, the information control program had entered its second phase all along the line, but had entered the third phase in but one instance—the Aachen newspaper, discussed earlier in this account. After the final division of Germany into Zones of Occupation, following the dissolution of the combined headquarters, Aachen fell in the British zone, PWD's successor in the American Zone thus took up the tasks of information control with all media still in the second, or overt phase.

The following statement of the status of Information control is as of the end of September, 1945. Although it does not fall legitimately into a recounting of the history of PWD/SHAEF, it must be recalled that the operations of ICD stemmed directly from the planning of PWD.

A. Radio

The operation of German radio in the U.S. Zone utilized high powered transmitters located at the strategic coverage points of Munich, Stuttgart and Frankfurt. Operation of transmitters of lower power was contemplated at Nürnberg, Kassel and Bremen.

When Allied troops arrived, the Munich transmitters had suffered relatively little damage; those at Stuttgart had been more heavily damaged by German demolition squads; the Frankfurt transmitters were completely demolished and PWD had provided new equipment. The Nürnberg transmitter was undamaged. Beyond this, land-lines between studios and transmitters and the studios themselves had undergone severe damage.

During the Occupation, up to the date of this report, ICD radio broadcasting took the following forms:

Initially, Radio Luxembourg operated on an $11^{1/2}$ hour daily schedule, which was progressively increased. On May 12, 1945, Radio Munich went on the air at 100 kilowatts. On June 3 Radio Stuttgart went on the air at 100 kilowatts. On June 2 Radio Frankfurt began transmissions using a one-kilowatt transmitter, later increased to 20 kilowatts. Eventually the power was to be 60 kilowatts.

Coverage of the American Zone in Germany was assured by the four stations noted above, operating on a network basis. Luxembourg remained the key station, initiating programs on a schedule of $13^{1/2}$ hours per day, of which ten hours were available to the local stations. Beyond the relayed programs the local stations orginated the following schedules: Munich $5^{1/2}$ hours on week days, nine hours on Sundays; Stuttgart $1^{1/2}$ hours on weekdays, $2^{1/2}$ hours on Sundays; Frankfurt four hours on weekdays, $8^{1/2}$ on Sundays.

These programs consisted of news, both world and local, comment on the news, re-educational programs, Military Government proclamations and instructions, English lessons, talks on literature and the drama, and the necessary musical interludes indispensable for acquiring and maintaining an audience.

Editorial and policy personnel of the various stations in Germany was entirely U.S. Germans were used as technicians, announcers, translators, writers and producers, but under strict supervision.

Planning for the future was toward removal of the seat of the network key station from Luxembourg to Frankfurt, where German personnel would be available in larger numbers than at Luxembourg. Further, it appeared highly appropriate that radio broadcasting for Germans should originate in Germany.

It was planned that responsibility for operation of German broadcasting under U.S. policy control in the American Zone be assigned to German authority early in 1946.

The following is quoted from the ICD report of September 22, 1945, describing outstanding problems facing the radio operation:

"The main outstanding problem is the constitution of German agencies to assume responsibilities of operation. The present plan is for each regional Chief Executive (three in the American Zone) to assume personal responsibility for the operating of the broadcasting station in his area, under Information Control direction. Collectively they will be responsible for the operations of the stations as a network. Whether or not this responsibility will continue into the indefinite future cannot now be determined. Eventual alternatives are: (1) a chartered company under a government franchise, (2) commercial broadcasting companies, (3) or a combination of (1) and (2).

In this connection it is pertinent to note that limitations on the number of broadcast frequencies in Germany preclude the establishment of competing radio services in the U.S. Zone in the standard broadcast band. As a result of the consequent complete monopoly, no plans for commercialization of German radio under present technical conditions have been considered. However, at such time as equipment may be available for broadcasting and receiving in the higher frequency bands (FM or AM) the present frequency limitations may be removed and competing services may be feasible. In that case, commercialization of all or part of radio in the U.S. Zone can be considered as long range policy.

The second important technical problem to date has been that of land lines linking the various stations. Now, however, the installation of lines connecting Frankfurt, Stuttgart, and Munich is imminent and it is hoped that those which will link Bremen, Kassel and Nürnberg to the network will not be long delayed. Network operations are desirable for the sake of the unity they give to output which for policy purposes should have Zone-wide distribution, and for the economy they effect in key editorial and production personnel. Relay by existing radio link from Radio Luxembourg is unsatisfactory and undependable.

A third problem is that of personnel — both U.S. and German. In making plans for the staffing of U.S.-operated stations by U.S. military and civilian personnel it was impossible to have foreknowledge of the redeployment program and the serious depletions it would bring about in staff of specialists assembled for Information Control. Similarly, the end of the war, uncertainty for the future, and reductions in income brought about by reductions in overtime and post allowances, have reduced the ranks of specialized civilian personnel.

On the other hand, key German personnel is not being unovered with anticipated degree of rapidity.

A further problem is one of radio supply, both from the broadcasting standpoint and that of the civilian receiver. Tubes for broadcasting transmitters are in short supply and those for receiving sets are practically non-existent. Currently, efforts are being made through Signal channels to have the necessary German type transmitter tubes manufactured in France or Switzerland. The manufacture of tubes and spare parts for radio receivers is under discussion. It will be necessary to establish a policy concerning the activation of tube and radio receiver parts manufacture in Germany or the import of such items from other countries.

The final problem is that of Quadripartite understanding on radio service for Germany.

B. Press

In the second phase of the PWD/ICD plan for control of German Information Services, overt Army newspapers were published in key cities. These were replaced, in city after city, by licensed newspapers published by acceptable Germans.

As of September 22, 1945, American Army overt newspapers still were being published in Augsburg (circulation 240,000); Bamberg (circulation 601,500); Berlin (circulation 604,000); Kassel (circulation 220,000); Munich (circulation 582,000); and Straubing (circulation 328,000). These papers were weeklies, save for the *Allgemeine Zeitung* in Berlin which appeared thrice weekly.

Meanwhile, since the dissolution of SHAEF, when the American Zone was without licensed newspapers, licensees had been approved in the following cities:

Frankfurt (circulation 415,000 twice weekly) Stuttgart (circulation 200,000)
Bremen (circulation 150,000) Marburg (circulation 15,000)
Heidelberg (circulation 200,000) Berlin (circulation 200,000).

Imminent were lincenses for Garmisch-Partenkirchen, Munich, Kassel and Wiesbaden. In Berlin, the overt paper continued publication on alternate days with the licensee paper.

The newsprint shortage still was the paramount problem and it limited licensee papers to two editions per week, save in Berlin where three were contemplated. Also, it limited papers to one per city. This second limitation increased the problem of assuring adequate outlet for all anti-Nazi German groups political, economic and religious. The problem was being met by directing that newspaper columns be open to all such groups, and by jointly licensing several individuals to publish a single newspaper. Thus, in the case of the *Frankfurter Rundschau*, the licensed group included a Catholic, a Communist, two Social Democrats, and two non-party members.

The overt and licensee newspapers were supplied with news by a service in German, operated by ICD and transmitted by radio teletype throughout the Zone from a central newsroom in Bad Nauheim. This German News Service (known in German as the Deutsche Allgemeine Nachrichten-Agentur, or DANA) replaced the Allied Press Service on September 6th. APS was the joint Anglo-American agency that previously had serviced PWD field operations. DANA's daily file totalled some 25,000 words of consolidated world and German news.

Under a new directive, licensee newspapers were to be permitted to obtain world news from any available source, and to enter upon negotiations with regular commercial agencies such as AP, UP, Reuter, etc., whenever those agencies should be in a position to provide service.

Beyond this, it was planned to license German groups to take over the internal German news service to be run cooperatively by the German licensed papers it served.

ICD looked toward elimination of all overt newspapers as soon as possible, but planned to continue to operate a Zone-wide overt paper to provide an official mouthpiece for the American occupation forces.

Under the terms of their licenses, German publishers were responsible for the integrity of their employees, and for the financial aspects of their enterprises under ICD auditing. Certain percentages of their net revenues were placed in blocked accounts to cover the cost of the DANA service, of newsprint allocations, etc. Beyond this, a certain percentage was so placed to cover rent and depreciation of requisitioned plant and facilities against eventual adjudication of ownership claims.

C. Publications

Under phase one of the German control plan, all publishing houses and book shops in Germany were closed. In the nearly five months between V-E Day and the end of September 1945, eight book publishers had been licensed in the American Zone. Of these, four were for publication of religious material, and the remainder were issued to general publishers.

The ICD plan provided for two types of permits to function in the information field. Individuals wishing to create material—to publish books, to publish newspapers, to produce films — were to be licensed. On the other hand, mere registration was to be required for individuals wishing to sell books, operate motion picture theaters, etc. Under this procedure, during the period when eight book publishers were licensed, 2800 book shops were registered in the American Zone.

The pressure to license book publishers was very strong, since there existed in Germany, in the months following the end of the war, an intense desire for information which had been withheld from the people for twelve years. The German people had ample time for reading, but there was very little available for them. With Nazi literature removed from book-sellers shelves, practically nothing remained.

In order to fulfill the need while the necessarily laborious process of vetting German publishers and German manuscripts proceeded, ICD embarked upon a second and temporary program. This involved publication of Allied and American books and articles to bridge the gap in the German people's understanding of the status of the world outside Nazi Germany since 1933. German translation rights were purchased by OWI for twenty American titles, and eigthy others were in process of negotiation. These were to be placed with suitable licensed publishers.

In the field of magazines, two special American magazines were being produced, "Heute," a picture-and-text periodical, and "Amerikanische Rundschau," a somewhat more weighty publication. Pressure was being applied toward licensing of German publishers of youth and women's magazines.

Book dealers and publishers declared that the following types of material were most needed by German readers:

(1) New school books, teachers' manuals, technical handbooks.
(2) Surveys of advances in science and applied science in foreign countries since 1933.
(3) A one-volume history of the United States.
(4) Travel books and descriptions of foreign countries.
(5) Books banned by the Nazis, such as those of Mann, Zweig, Undset, Wasserman, etc.
(6) Books of religion and philosophy.
(7) Biographies free from propaganda.
(8) Objective histories of the last twelve years.

Work had begun on the reconstitution of a free publishers trade organization. A branch of the Boersenverein was being etablished at Wiesbaden. The Boersenverein formerly was the central coordinating agency for the entire German book trade and this central organization, it was expected, would simplify the task of supplying licensed publishers with ideas, advising them with regard to priorities in publication, and preventing two or more publishers from publishing the same or similar texts. This last was regarded as being a highly important aid in economizing on use of the scanty paper stocks.

D. Films, Theaters, Music

1. *Films.* In phase one, all motion picture theaters were closed, and all available German films impounded. It had been the original PWD/SHAEF plan to proceed slowly with the reopening of the theaters, but as time went on, under pressure of demand and in view of the more liberal policy of the other Allies, ICD proceeded at a progressively accelerated pace in the registration of theater owners. By the end of September, some 50 movie theaters had been registered in the American Zone. This figure represented a relatively low proportion of the pre-war movie theaters in the area, but it must be borne in mind that many theaters had been destroyed or damaged beyond immediate repair, and that

many of the remaining theaters were requisitioned by Special Services for use of American troops.

The registered film theaters were provided with selected U.S. features, documentaries and shorts, as well as a joint Anglo-American weekly newsreel. PWD officers had collaborated with OWI in production of a film on Nazi concentration camps, and ICD continued its treatment of including atrocity sequences in film showings.

The Bavaria Filmkunst Studios near Munich were under requisition by ICD, where the weekly newsreel was produced.

2. *Theaters.* The major effort in this field, as in others, was toward licensing of suitable producers and obtaining rights to American plays. Some twenty producers had been licensed by the end of September.

3. *Music.* Musical performances by orchestras and soloists were increasingly frequent in the American Zone, and six symphony orchestras had been organized. The were: Frankfurt-Stuttgart (joint), Munich, Heidelberg, Ober-Hesse, Nürnberg, and Marburg-Kassel (joint).

The whole problem of music control was among the most difficult-facing ICD. It involved the question: just how political is music? And the further question: what are the political connotations of licensing a symphony conductor who performed under the Nazi regime, but who was not an active Nazi. These questions, and their corollaries, were decided in each case on its merits, distilled from exhaustive investigations of the circumstances. In general, ICD did not proscribe any save Nazi party or Wehrmacht songs. It did not proscribe performances of Wagner, despite the association of his music with Hitler. It did, however, discourage Wagner Festivals.

E. Quadripartite Problems

In every medium of ICD operation, the problems of understandings and agreements among the four occupying powers loomed ever more vital in the achievement of comon aims.

In general, these problems were most apparent in Berlin, where the four powers—America, Britain, Russia, France—each controlled a district of the city, but by extension the same problems were to be found in the four Zones throughout the country.

In Berlin, attempts were being made late in September to arrive at agreements on uniform policies governing exhibition of films, musical performances, etc., as well as on the paramount problem of use of the "Berlin Tegel" radio transmitter. This transmitter was under control of the Russians, und was being used both as the key station for the entire Russian Zone, and for local Berlin coverage. The aim of continuing conferences was toward quadripartite use of the transmitter at certain hours for local Berlin service.

In the field of news, exchange of files among the four zones was already a reality, making it possible for newspapers in any Zone to publish internal German news from all parts of the country.

ICD Films sub-section was proposing production of a weekly newsreel on a quadripartite level; pool of rawstock and chemical supplies; organization of a quadripartite film censorship board; exchange of films on a parity basis until the establishment of commercial distributors in Germany, and the production of two dozen or more documentaries at the Bavarian Filmkunst Studios, the work to be done by German civilians under quadripartite supervision.

APPENDIX "A"

SHAEF Operation Memorandum No. 8

The PWD Charter

SUPREME HEADQUARTERS ALLIED EXPEDITIONARY FORCE

OPERATION MEMORANDUM, NUMBER 8   11 March 1944

Psychological Warfare

1. OBJECT

The object of this memorandum is to define the responsibilities for the control, coordination, and operation of Psychological Warfare within the Allied Expeditionary Force.

2. DEFINITION

Psychological Warfare is the dissemination of propaganda designed to undermine the enemy's will to resist, demoralize his forces and sustain the morale of our supporters.

3. CLASSES OF PROPAGANDA

1. Propaganda can be broadly divided into three interdependent and closely related classes, as follows:—
   a. Strategic Propaganda directed on enemy and enemy-occupied countries. Such propaganda has the double task of undermining the enemy's will to resist and sustaning the morale of our supporters.
   b. Combat (or Tactical) Propaganda conducted against the enemy forces in the forward areas and towards the population immediately behind the enemy lines.
   c. Consolidation Propaganda conducted towards the civil population in the rear areas, with a view to ensuring friendly cooperation, particulary in restoring essential services, and to creating opinion favourable to the war and post-war aims of the United Nations.

4. STRATEGIC PROPAGANDA

   a. Strategic Propaganda is carried out by the US. Office of War Information (O.W.I.), the BRITISH Political Warfare Executive (P.W.E.), the BRITISH Ministry of Information (M.O.I.), and the Morale Operation (M.O.) Branch of the US.Office of Strategic Services (O.S.S.). These agencies operate under joint O.W.I.-P.W.E. directives approved by the Combined Chiefs of Staff, and in emergency under temporary directives issued by the LONDON Propaganda Co-ordinating Committee (L.P.C.).
   b. The Psychological Warfare Branch of G-6 (P & PW) Division, at Supreme Headquarters, ensures that these directives are in keeping with the plans of the Supreme Commander and co-ordinates the activities of the various agencies insofar as they affect that part of the EUROPEAN sphere for which the Supreme Commander is responsible.
   c. Strategic Propaganda activieties include:

   (1) Radio broadcasts   (3) Agents
   (2) Leaflets   (4) Rumors

5. COMBAT PROPAGANDA

   a. Gombat propaganda includes the following activities:

   (1) Political Survey (Intelligence) and other   (3) Monitoring Service.
        methods of collecting Psychological   (4) Mobile public address system.
        Warfare information.   (5) Tactical leaflets.
   (2) Mobile broadcasting units.   (6) Field Printing.

   b. Combat Propaganda will be confined within the terms of directives issued by Supreme Headquarters, Allied Expeditionary Force, to Army Groups and, as necessary, to Allied Naval Expeditionary Force and Allied Expeditionary Air Force.
   c. In order to execute Psychological Warfare Plans prepared under these directives,

Army Groups will raise, administer and operate Psychological Warfare Field Operational Units capable of carrying out the activities listed in pargr. 5 a above.

6. CONSOLIDATION PROPAGANDA

a. Consolidation Propaganda will normally be carried out by Supreme Headquarters, Allied Expeditionary Force. When desirable and practicable, tasks will be decentralized to Army Groups under special directives.

b. Consolidation Propaganda includes the following activities:—
   (1) Political Survey (Intelligence) and other methods of collecting Psychological Warfare Intelligence.
   (2) Operation or control and servicing of local press.
   (3) Operation or control and servicing of broadcasting stations.
   (4) Operation or control and servicing of cinemas.
   (5) Distribution of propaganda literature and displays.
   (6) Liaison on Psychological Warfare matters.

7. CONTROL

a. The successful outcome of Psychological Warfare demands centralized control and coordination of propaganda themes and aims. Any departure from this principle can only lead to ineffective or disastrous results.

b. Whenever a specific use of propaganda is desired by a subordinate commander, the Psychological Warfare Branch at the appropriate headquarters will be consulted as to the type or line of propaganda to be used.

c. Any departure required by Commanders-in-Chief (Commanding Generals) Army Groups or subordinate commanders from the terms of directives issued to them will be refered to and receive the prior concurrence of Supreme Headquarters.

d. Army Groups will ensure that all possible assistance is given to the execution of approved Psychological Warfare Plans. Requests for air assistance will be made by Army Groups and Armies to their associated Air Forces. Requests for naval assistance will be made through Supreme Headquarters, Allied Expeditionary Force, to Allied Naval Expeditionary Force.

OFFICIAL:	By command of General EISENHOWER:
H. R. BULL,	W. B. SMITH,
Major General G.S.C.	Lieutenant General, U.S. Army,
Assistent Chief of Staff, G-3.	Chief of Staff.

APPENDIX "B"

Voice of SHAEF Texts

(Designed in the first instance for use on the Anglo-American radio directed toward the continent, these messages formed the basis for psychological warfare activities in all media. Through them it is possible to trace the progress of the strategic planning of the campaign in Northwestern Europe from D-Day onwards.)

The VOICE of SHAEF texts which are printed on the following pages were produced at frequent intervals throughout the campaign. They represented the underlying operational policy of psychological warfare in Northwestern Europe.

PWD recognized the strong possibility that the enemy would attempt to confuse the various audiences on the continent by spurious broadcasts from his own transmitters. Therefore, a rather intricate method was devised in order to authenticate the genuine Voice of SHAEF broadcasts.

In reproducing Voice of SHAEF No. 1, the complete text, with lead-in and lead-out, is given. In all the others, in order to conserve space, only the operational message is reproduced. In every case, however, the recorded lead-in and lead-out, done by the same voices, were used.

It is to be understood by the reader that these broadcasts were made in all of the appropriate European languages, plus English.

SHAEF Voice No. 68
April 20, 1945

The following message is addressed to Russian and Polish Nationals in the gap between the Anglo-American and Russian Armies.

1. Do not move West. Stay where you are. In a few days the gap between the liberating armies from the West and from the East will be closed.

When the armies link up they will make arrangements for your return home.

If you move West now you will delay your return home. By staying where you are you speed up your return home.

2. Keep discipline. Suppress pillaging and looting. Until the Allied armies reach you, you have the right to obtain from the German authorities food and lodging. Do this in an orderly way. Elect leaders who will make the arrangements with the Germans. Disorderly pillaging and looting only delays the Allied advance.

When the Allied armies reach you they will arrange for your feeding and housing. Leaders of groups must therefore report immediately to Allied authorities. They will then receive instructions about feeding and housing.

SHAEF Voice No. 69
April 21, 1945

The following message is adressed to Prisoners-of-War, Foreign Workers and Deportees.

A. Before you are liberated:

1. Stay where yo are. Take shelter and await the Allied armies.
2. Form small groups of your own nationality and elect leaders.
3. Elected leaders should arrange with German local authorities for food and lodging for their group. They should be on the look-out for Fascist and German Agents who are trying to foment disorder in order to delay the Allied armies.
4. Elected leaders should do everything to prevent the destruction of industrial plant machinery, office equipment, documents and drawings, either by the Germans or by the liberated workers. These are required to fight the Germans and for the reconstruction of Europe after the war.

B. When you are liberated:

1. Do not move out of the district—wait for orders.
2. Keep discipline in your groups. Obey your elected leaders.
3. Leaders should report to Allied military authorities immediately and follow their orders.
4. Stay off main roads used by military traffic.
5. Hand in all weapons and ammunition. Violations will be punished under Military Law. It is the special responsibility of leaders of groups to see that this is done as soon as possible.
6. Let your behaviour be a credit to your National honour. Disorder, looting or sabotage will not be tolerated. Violations will be punshed under military law.
7. As soon as Military operations permit you will be directed to Assembly Centres to prepare for your return home.
8. Patience and discipline will hasten your return.

SHAEF Voice No. 70
April 24, 1945

The following message is addressed to the Garrison of Festung Holland.

It is well known to you that four and a half million Dutch civilians are starving to death behind your lines.

It is well known to you that the German Government has ceased to exercise effective authority over anything except a few pockets of resistance in Germany.

It is well known to you that the German Army has ceased to exist as an integrated fighting force.

Despite these facts you are still obeying the criminal order for resistance to the last. The full consequence of your resistance will be death by starvation of thousands of Dutch civilians and still more widespread devastation of Holland.

To alleviate the sufferings of the Dutch population while the final phase of the battle proceeds, the Supreme Commander has given orders that food should be flown in and dropped to the Dutch civilian population. This food will be carried in large numbers of aircraft of all types operating both day and night. These aircraft will be fulfilling not a mission of war but a mission of relief to suffering civilians. They will fly in low and will undertake no acts which will in any way affect operations. There will be no bombing, strafing or any other offensive action.

The Supreme Commander has therefore authorised the following instructions to you:—

1. Any attempt to oppose the Allied aircraft bringing food to the Dutch civilians or to prevent them completing their mission of relief is a crime against humanity. Those who commit this crime either by giving the order to fire on your aircraft or by carrying it out must expect to bear the full consequences when the day of reckoning comes.

2. Any attempt to deprive the Dutch civilians of the food which the Allies will drop to them will also be regarded as a crime against humanity for which the perpetrators must bear the full consequences.

3. All of you should in your own self-interest do all that is possible to help in the distribution of this food to the Dutch civilians.

That ends this message dated 24th April 1945 issued by Supreme Headquarters, Allied Expeditionary Force, on the authority of the Supreme Commander, addressed to the Garrison of Festung Holland.

SHAEF Voice No. 71
April 25, 1945

(To be broadcast in CZECH and GERMAN, interrupting other transmissions when necessary, and cross-reported in other languages. The warning should be repeated intermittently until 1100 DBST)

The following warning is issued from Supreme Headquarters, Allied Expeditionary Force.

WARNING: Allied bombers are out in great strength today. Their destination may be the Skoda works. Skoda workers get out and stay out till the afternoon.

SHAEF Voice No. 73
April 29, 1945

1. On 24th April, 1945, a message was issued by Supreme Headquarters, Allied Expeditionary Force, on the authority of the Supreme Commander, addressed to the people of Occupied Holland. It stated that the people of Occupied Holland might expect deliveries of food dropped by aircraft. You were warned to watch out for these aircraft and organize yourselves under your responsible leaders into watching and collecting parties. When you heard our aircraft, you were warned that you must take shelter away from the areas in which dropping might occur. You were instructed to post observers at pre-arranged points to note where the packages landed, and you were told to distribute the food fairly. These instructions have now been altered. The collection and distribution will now be made by your own officials. I repeat—the collection and distribution will now be made by your own officials.

2. The food-carrying aircraft will first drop bright colored flares to guide them. These flares will burst in the air and will be colored red or green. The flares will make a distinctive noise while they are falling. These red or green flares are not bombs. I repeat—these red or green flares are not bombs.

3. These aircraft will be on their way the moment the weather is suitable. These aircraft will be carrying food not bombs—I repeat, they will be carrying food not bombs.

That ends this message dated 29th April, 1945, issued by Supreme Headquarters Allied Expeditionary Force, on the authority of the Supreme Commander, addressed to the people of Ocupied Holland.

SHAEF Voice No. 74
April 30, 1945

The German authorities have offered to leave behind all Prisoners of War of Allied Nations in camps which they abandon in the face of the Allies' advance. The Governments of the United States of America, Great Britain, the Union of Soviet Socialist Republics and France have accepted this offer.

It has not been possible for the German authorities to transmit this information to all of this commanders in the field. It is therefore broadcast in this manner so that all German commanders concerned may know of this agreement.

The Supreme Commander expects that all German commanders shall carry out their part of this agreement and will hold them strictly accountable for any violation thereof.

SHAEF Voice No. 77
May 9, 1945

The following are instructions to officers and men of the Wehrmacht in Norway:—

The German armed forces in Norway have surrendered unconditionally. Your duty as soldiers is clear. Your orders for the present are as follows:—

1. Maintain your discipline. Obey the orders of your commanders.
2. Remain with your units.
3. Restrain and detain any undisciplined elements among you who may harm the Norwegian people. You are warned that you will be held responsible individually and collectively for any injury to Norwegian persons and any damage to Norwegian property.
4. The further orders of the Allied Supreme Commander will be transmitted to you through your own commander and by Allied leaflets and radio.

BY ORDER OF THE SUPREME COMMANDER
OF THE ALLIED EXPEDITIONARY FORCE

SHAEF Voice No. 78
May 10, 1945

Here is a special Order of the Day from General Eisenhower, the Supreme Commander, to the Resistance Forces of France, Belgium, Holland, Denmark and Norway:—

The Germans who invaded, occupied and plundered your homelands have been finally defeated by the forces of the United Nations, and your countries have now been liberated by the combined efforts of all the forces under my command.

Not least among these forces I count the members of Resistance, who for so long have devoted themselves unflinchingly to the task of overthrowing the common enemy. Constantly informed of your activity, I have watched your efforts with admiration.

I know how hard your task has been. I know how many of you have been imprisoned, tortured and murdered. Inadequately armed and in the midst of a savage and ruthless enemy you have fought on month after month, year after year, regardless of the disappointment you have suffered and of the danger you have undergone.

Some of you have waged open warfare against the enemy: others have had to undergo the strain of carrying on clandestine activities, which by their nature have had to remain unnoticed and apparently unrewarded by your comrades in arms; for most of you sole reward has been the knowledge that you have by your efforts helped to rid your homeland of a hated enemy.

In this great hour of victory, as your Supreme Commander, I thank you, forces of Resistance, for your discipline, for your great courage, and for inestimable service to the Allied cause and to the future of all freedom-loving peoples.

SHAEF Voice No. 79
May 10, 1945

The following message to the people of Norway is issued by the Supreme Commander, Allied Expeditionary Force.

Our united efforts have brought complete victory over the common German enemy Our great task has been achieved, not only by the valour and self-sacrifice of the fighting men of the free Nations, but also by the great spirit of resistance which men and women in countries overrun by the Nazis have sustained through the long hard years of repression.

You, the people of NORWAY, have been a great example to us fighting the Nazis on all fronts. Your struggle and your heavy sacrifices during the years of occupation will live brightly in the pages of your history, and in the memory of generations of free men to come.

Norwegian, British and American forces under my Supreme Command are in NORWAY, in order to re-establish Norwegian sovereignty, to disarm and control the forces of the enemy still in Norway, and to help in speeding up the return of normal Norwegian conditions of order and decency. As soon as their main task of controlling the enemy forces has been accomplished, these forces who are not Norwegian will be withdrawn from Norway for duties elsewhere.

After five years of enemy ocupation, the return to normal conditions will not be accomplished in a day You will find yourselves facing many difficulties and hardships for some time to come. But whatever the temporary difficulties, NORWAY will be free.

The speedy accomplishment of the task of Allied Forces in NORWAY will greatly depend on your cooperation. I ask you to do all you can to help them, as they will do all they can to help you.

I am confident that when the time comes for Allied soldiers to leave your country, they will take with them your good will and friendship. Thus you and they will contribute towards the fellowship and community of free Nations, for which our long struggle has ben fought.

SHAEF Voice No. 80
May 13, 1945

Here are instructions to Allied prisoners-of-war and Allied nationals in Norway:
1. The German Armed Forces in Norway have surrendered.
2. Plans of the Allied Governments who care for you and who return you to your country are ready and will be put into force as soon as possible.
3. These plans will be carried out with much greater speed if you obey my instructions. Obedience will hasten your return home. Disobedience will mean delay and unnecessary hardship for you.
4. These are my instructions to you:
   (a) Stay where you are. The frontiers are closed.
   (b) Organise yourselves into groups with your own leaders, if you have not already done so.
5. Representatives of your Governments are now on their way to make contact with you and to carry out, with your help, the plans prepared for your return.
6. I have ordered the German authorities to supply you with food, shelter, clothing and medical care.

Stay where you are and await further instructions.

SHAEF Voice No. 81
May 15, 1945

The following message is addressed to the people of Holland:—

Dutch civilians. In order to facilitate the distribution of foodstuffs and supplies essential for your own well being, your are urgently requested to stay off all main highways and roads. The excessive circulation of civilians on roads is delaying the distribution of food and the movement of Allied troops. We repeat: for your own good, civilians must stay off all main highways and roads.

APPENDIX "C"
Military Government Talks

Series on Military Government of Germany No. 11
(Open and close with set formula, as in Nr. 1)

1. Works of art and objects of scientific or historical importance which have been looted by Germany from Allied countries will be recovered and restored to their rightful owners and it is the responsibility of every German who wishes to make restitution for the wrongs done by his country to assist in their location and delivery to the Military Government.
2. All sales and movements of such objects be forbidden and destruction or concealment of them will be severely punished.
3. Every effort will be made to avoid, as far as military necessity allows damage to any building, monument, document or other object of cultural, artistic, archaeological, or historical value, which rightfully belongs to Germans.
4. The Military Government has compiled a list of monuments which must not be used for military purposes unless military necessity requires the Commander on the spot to make an exception. Commanders will, in general, put these buildings out-of-bounds for Allied troops.
5. Steps will be taken to preserve in safekeeping all German records, documents and archives of value.
6. It is the responsibility of Germans to refuse to take part in the policy of "scorched earth," which the Nazis plan to carry out. "Scorched earth" implies a policy in connection with "retreat." Where are the Germans retreating to?

Series on Military Government of Germany No. 12
(Open and close with set formula, as in No. 1)

1. When circumstances permit German workers will be allowed to form democratic trade unions to replace the Nazi-controlled Labour Front and other Party organisations, which will be abolished at once. All forms of free economic association and combination among workers will be permitted, provided that they do not assume any political or militaristic complexion.
2. The restoration of this fundamental right which the Nazis abrogated will enable workers to embark upon collective bargaining with employers but strikes threatening military security, directly or indirectly, will be prohibited. So will lock-outs.
3. For the time being, you will maintain your limits on wages under the most recent German regulations.
4. All deductions of pay at the source or collections from workers for the benefit of the NSDAP or any of its affiliated dissolved organisations will cease. Deductions of payments for social insurance, unemployment insurance, workmen's compensation, or normal Reich taxes will be continued.
5. Existing laws, decrees and regulations regarding the registration of labour will continue otherwise as emergency measures. That is to say, workers must have their employment status examined and recorded, and their work books verified and re-registered. All workers, male or female, in employment or unemployed, must report to the Labour Office in the area where they are living for registration or re-registration.
6. The civilian labour requirements of the Military Forces will be given the first priority, but due recognition will be given to the retention of key civilians in public services, utilities or essential industries. Any surplus labour will be used for work on such tasks as are approved by the Military Government.

Series on Military Government of Germany No. 13
(Open and close with set formula, as in No. 1)

1. It is the policy of the Supreme Commander to eradicate Nazism and German militarism in all their aspects from the German educational system. All active Nazis and ardent Nazi sympathizers and militarists will be removed from educational positions and all educational institutions (except boarding schools and orphanages) will be closed until Nazism has been eliminated.
2. Elementary schools will first be reopened. School supplies and facilities must be furnished from your own resources. The existing German educational system, subject

to Military Government control, will be employed as far as possible after purging of Nazi and militaristic elements. No appointment or reinstatement made to any position in the German educational system will be considered permanent.

3. Steps to reopen secondary schools and higher German educational institutions will be taken as soon as practicable. You will be directed to make emergency repairs to school buildings.

4. All Nazi Party organisations and their affiliates in schools, all special Nazi schools (including Adolph-Hitler-Schulen, Napolas, and Ordensburgen), all Nazi Youth organisations (including Jungvolk, Hitler-Jugend, Jungmädel and Bund Deutscher Mädel) and the Nazi adult education organisation (Deutsches Volksbildungswerk) will be abolished. New organisations may not be founded without permission of Military Government.

5. German teachers will be instructed to eliminate from their teaching anything which—

(a) Glorifies militarism, expounds the practice of war or of mobilisation and preparation for war, whether in the scientific, economic or industrial fields or the study of military geography.

(b) Seeks to propagate, revive or justify the doctrines of Nazism or to extol the achievements of Nazi leaders.

(c) Favours a policy of driscrimination on grounds of race or religion.

(d) Is hostile to, or seeks to disturb, the relations beween any of the United Nations. Any infringement of these provisions will be cause for immediate dismissal and punishment.

6. Military Government will not intervene in questions of denominational control of German schools or religious instruction in German schools except insofar as may be necessary to insure that religious instruction and the administration of such schools conform to such regulations as are or may be established for all subjects and all schools.

APPENDIX "D"

Standing Directive for Psychological Warfare against Members of the German Armed Forces

June 1944.

Scope and Purpose of this Directive

1. This Standing Directive lays down the general lines to be followed in all forms of white propaganda directed to German armed forces in the West. It is intended as a Standing Directive, valid both before and after D-day. It will be supplemented from time to time by special directives, as well as by the weekly Central Directive prepared by PWE/OWI in collaboration with PWD/SHAEF. Unless expressly stated, however, these directives should be regarded as supplementary to and not as cancelling the present Standing Directive, which has the approval of PWE/OWI.

2. The Moscow Declaration laid down the principle that the individual would be held responsible for his war crimes. This applies equally to the soldier and to the civilian; a uniform neither aggravates nor mitigates the guilt of the individual, thus the Declaration ruled out the suggestion of mass reprisals.

3. But it has also been made clear by our Governments that they are determined to destroy not only the Nazi system, but the concept of the Wehrmacht, which has been both the initiator and the willing instrument of recurring German attempts to dominate other peoples. Nothing in the implementation of this directive must compromise that issue.

4. It is recognised that in the execution of Psychological Warfare it is a fundamental principle not to antagonise the audience. Direct denunciation or direct offence against known susceptibilities will therefore be avoided in all Psychological Warfare against the enemy armed forces. On the other hand nothing will be done to encourage or condone the concept of German militarism and the attitudes of mind behind it, both of which we are pleged to destroy.

General Considerations

5. Psychological Warfare is not a magic substitute for physical battle, but an auxiliary to it. By attacking the fighting morale of the enemy, it aims at (a) reducing the cost of the physical battle and (b) rendering the enemy easier to handle after surrender.

6. The conduct of Psychological Warfare therefore forms part of the conduct of military operations, and must be co-ordinated with that of other arms of war. It is the task of Psychological Warfare to assist the Supreme Commander in fulfilling his mission against the enemy with the most economical use of troops and equiment.

7. The use of Psychological Warfare in military operations must however be strictly subordinated to the long-term policy of our Governments, in the sense that nothing must be done with the object of undermining fighting morale during operations which would prejudice Government policy to Germany after the war. To this end, this Standing Directive for Psychological Warfare during operations is preceded by a summary of standing high policy directives.

8. These high policy directives define not the strategy of the campaign which Psychological Warfare will conduct against German fighting morale, but the limits within which it must, for policy reasons, be confined.

Standing High Policy Directives

9. No specific promises will be made concerning the treatment of Germany after the war, other than those expressly made by Government spokesmen. In particular there must be no suggestion that the Atlantic Charter applies to Germany by right.

10. On no account must there be any suggestion or implication:—
    (I) that we recognise any claim of the German Army to be absolved from its full share of responsibility for German aggression on the grounds that its part is merely professional and non-political and that it does no more than obey orders;
    (II) that we recognise the possibility of divorcing the "fighting war" from the atrocities which the German soldier has committed or condoned, e.g. the taking and shooting of hostages and the murder of prisoners;
    (III) that we would be prepared to allow German militarism to survive in any form.

11. The following are the points on which our Governments have committed themselves:
    (a) Demilitarisation of Germany.
    (b) Punishment of war criminals.
    (c) Liberation of territories overrun by Nazi-Germany, including Austria.
    (d) Occupation of Germany
    (e) Destruction of Nazism and German Militarism.
    (f) Prevention of such economic distress in Germany as will be detrimental to the rest of the world.
    (g) Ultimate restoration of Germany to a place "in the world family of democratic nations".

The key quotations on these points are given in Annexe I. Note that (d), (f) and (g) are only general commitments, and may not be elaborated in Psychological Warfare unless and until specific Government statements are forthcoming on these points.

Appreciation of Strength and Weakness of German Fighting Morale with Special Reference to Psychological Warfare

Note: Except where specifically stated the following generalisations apply to the German Army; not to the Air Force or Navy.

12. **Strong Points.**
    (I) *The Habit of Discipline.* The habit of uncritical obedience to authority, rather than any ruthless enforcement of discipline from above, remains the strongest factor in German morale today. This factor may not decrease sharply until the German Army as a whole is broken on the battlefield, since the retreats and defensive battles to which the Wehrmacht is now committed automatically place greater reliance on higher authority than offensive campaigns of the 1940 type.
    (II) *Comradeship.* The ideal of comradeship has been keenly cultivated in the German Army, particularly since 1933. The German NCO forms a transitional

stage between soldier status and officer status, a fact which strengthens this sense of comradeship. It has furthermore been immensely deepened by the Russian campaign.

(III) *Professional Pride.* The average German's conviction that the best life is the soldier's life, plus the social fact that the highest calling in Germany is the soldier's calling, constitutes a great source of strength.

Added to this the German soldier, and often the non-German soldier serving in the Wehrmacht, is convinced:—

(a) that he is privileged to be serving in the finest Army in the world, permeated with a code of soldierly honour which rules him and his officers alike;
(b) that the Wehrmacht is the embodiment of the highest physical and spiritual attainments of German culture;
(c) that the Wehrmacht is therefore the *non-political* guardian of the future of the German race;
(d) that as a fighting machine German "quality" can *probably* succeed in throwing back both Anglo-American and Russian "quantity."

(IV) *Material Interests.* The German Army represents, for the reasons stated in sub-paragr. (III) above, an honoured career with considerable material benefits. (Pay allowances and especially food are good compared with civilian standards in Germany.) Thousands of officers (especially those of junior and field rank) and tens of thousands of NCOs (particularly in specialist trades) have signed on not simply for the duration, but for periods varying from 7—14 years, or longer, and are fighting not only to preserve the German Army as a war machine, but as a means of livelihood.

(V) *The Bolshevik Bogey.* The guilty fear of Russian vengeance, linked with the Teuton dislike of the Slav and general fear of Bolshevism, has convinced the average German soldier that "anything is better than defeat in the East".

German propaganda has deliberately enlarged and intensified this fear, in the following ways:—

(a) It has largely succeeded in persuading the soldier that the Anglo-Americans are so dominated by the Bolshevik Colossus that they would be powerless to save Germany.
(b) It has filled the gap created by the absence of specific United Nations policy to Germany with atrocity stories of forced labour in Russia castration, deportation, etc.

(VI) *The Rewards of Victory in the West.* Learning from Mr. Churchill in 1940, the High Command has deliberately capitalized the threat of invasion from the West. It has:—

(a) argued that, if the Anglo-American threat can be frustrated or confined, the German Armies can be switched to the East. This argument has been used to justify the retreats in the East.
(b) argued that a defensive victory in the West will form the basis for the speedy conclusion of a "compromise peace" either with the West or with the East, which would in fact be a German victory.
(c) exploited the bombing of Germany to persuade the soldier that his only hope of regaining what he has lost lies in a German victory in the West.
(d) succeeded in convincing the German soldier that for these reasons one last tremendous effort must and can be made.

(VII) *Summary.*

(a) Taken by and large, it must be accepted that the German High Command has rendered the Army largely immune to the two Psychological Warfare campaigns which proved effective in 1918, i.e. Bolshevist propaganda, leading to soldiers and workers' councils; and democratic propaganda, leading to a revolt of the civilian under arms against the professional soldier.

We should assume that the German Army in the West will, like von Arnim's Army in Tunisia, fight on *as a whole* until it collapses *as a whole*. Indeed defeatism is more widespread at the top than at the bottom.

(b) The High Command has succeeded in actually raising fighting morale during the winter.

(c) For the reason outlined in sub-paragr. (I) above, no propaganda directed at the frontline German soldier is likely to be effective unless it sounds and looks more positive and authoritative than his own Army Order forbidding him to listen to it.

(d) For the reasons outlined in sub-paragr. (II) and (III) above, there is little prospect of dividing the German Army *internally*—i.e. setting men against officers. Furthermore, no propaganda aiming at inducing the surrender of German troops is likely to succeed unless it meets the fundamental objection that by surrender the individual is letting down his comrades.

13. **Weak Points.**

(I) *The Shaken Myth of Invincibility*. The long series of defeats suffered by the Wehrmacht in the Mediterranean and in Russia have shaken—but by no means shattered—the German soldier's faith in the mystic invincibility of German arms which carried his fighting morale up to a high tide of fanaticism in June, 1940. Within this general uneasiness are other specific doubts:

(a) *Doubts about the Fuhrer*. Allied propaganda that disasters such as Stalingrad, Tunisia, the Ukraine battle, and the Crimea, were largely due to the prestige policy of hanging on too long to too much, has gone home. Many German soldiers today feel that military operations are being dictated by political and often party considerations. The permeation of the OKW, and of the General Staff, with party generals, (notably the C. of S. Zeitzler) is largely blamed for this.

Note: At present, the average soldier, despite an awareness that he has made serious mistakes, is not inclined to blame Hitler, as the generals and other informed persons already do. Hitler is still his lucky talisman. Göring is also to some extent shielded. Of the German leaders, Himmler, Goebbels, and Ley, are the most unpopular. Generally speaking, "The System" or the "Party bosses" are the commonest scapegoat.

(b) *Doubts about Equipment*. German Army Equipment is good, and the German soldier knows it. But his battle experience since 1941 has given him painful proof that, in some respects at least, Allied equipment is not only more plentiful, but better. (Allied MT in Africa, Russian PAK, Russian medium tanks in the East and Allied fighter planes on all fronts are examples.)

The present „Wunderwaffe" vogue is in part a wishful thinking reaction to this.

(c) *Doubts about the News*. Despite intense efforts by the High Command, it has not succeeded in making the German soldier accept unquestioningly its interpretation of events. Most German soldiers, when they get the opportunity, read or listen to Anglo-American propaganda and try to find a truth halfway between their own communiques and ours. They assume that "everything is propaganda" and that they, as intelligent people, can read between the lines. Without knowing it, they are of course steeped in Nazi propaganda. They regard as "propaganda lies" such facts as that Germany invaded Poland, or that England has some highly developed social services. They have the useful faculty of forgetting any facts inconvenient to their superiors and believing they were invented by Anglo-American propaganda. Their outlook is formed however not by the direct output of the Propaganda Ministry, but by the educational and propaganda activities of the Wehrmacht. Nevertheless they are open to any propaganda which does not sound or read like "propaganda", and does not offend their sense of "soldierly honour". Unconsciously still, but actively, the German soldier craves for an excuse to stop the useless slaughter which leaves his honour as a German soldier unscathed, and puts the blame on someone or something outside the Wehrmacht. He needs in brief (I) facts, which seem to him to be objective, showing that despite the courage of the Wehrmacht, someone at home has lost the war for Germany; (II) a picture of the future which portrays death and destruction for "the betrayers of Germany" and survival for the German people.

Evidence for the above analysis is provided by the growing success of (a) Free German Committee broadcasts from Moscow, headed by General Seydlitz, and (b) Radio Calais. Both these transmissions seem to assume an analysis of German fighting morale similar to that above.

(d) *Doubts about the Luftwaffe.* Moreover, the *Air War* brings with it a cause of friction between the Air Force and the Army. German soldiers are beginning to talk like many British soldiers in 1940. This friction, and the resulting blame on "the authorities" is a real if minor chink in German fighting morale.

All these factors are important in that they provide the soldier with scapegoats for his decline in fortune, and when things go wrong the Germans natural reaction is: "I have been betrayed."

(II) *Manpower.* This is perhaps the main *operational* worry of the German soldier. He is disturbed by the enormous losses in men and material which he knows the battles in Russia have cost the Wehrmacht. This uneasiness is heightened by the Allied propaganda barrage on this theme, contrasted with the silence of his own authorities, a silence all the more significant when it persists even under the new OKW policy of simulating complete frankness on operational matters. This general manpower worry breaks down into other specific ones:

(a) The worry that, because of manpower troubles, the ranks of the Wehrmacht are being increasingly filled with foreigners of some twenty nationalities, and that the quality of the army is therefore in danger of "pollution."

(b) The worry that, with almost every one of its field divisions committed already to actual or potential battle-fields, the German Army has no effective central reserve to sustain it.

Both (a) and (b) above apply with particular force to the target of this paper—the German forces in the West. These troops have in their own formations large numbers of foreigners; and most of these divisions have had proof, by their own experience, of being switched from West to East and back, that no uncommitted central reserve exists. The great volume of German counter propaganda on this point is further evidence of its importance.

(III) *A War Gone Wrong.* In building up the picture of the chivalrous Wehrmacht in deadly battle against Bolshevism, the High Command inevitably raises in the German soldier's mind the question why Germany is fighting Britain and America, especially since Hitler denounced in *Mein Kampf* the fatal mistake of the two front war. The High Command seeks to answer this question by denouncing Anglo-American impotence and arguing that the Jews of Wall Street and the City of London are in conspiracy with the Kremlin. But this argument does not quell a deep uneasiness.

There is also a feeling in the German soldier's mind that the defensive battles which he is now forced to fight are not the battles for which he was trained, nor the battles for which his equipment was designed. There is evidence that the OKW had great trouble, during 1943, in converting officers and men to the technique of the defensive battle which their previous training had largely neglected.

The fear of isolation, a feature of what the Germans used to ridicule as "Maginot mindedness", is likely to be at its strongest among coastal formations in the West. They are particularly liable to the anxiety lest they be sacrificed as "human landmines".

(IV) *Loss of Honour.* An increasing number of soldiers are aware of, and uncomfortable about:—

(a) atrocities, especially in Russia. They naturally want to push the blame on to the SS., or simply "those in authority".

(b) the hostility of the occupied territories, including "Nordic" countries like Norway. The German wants to be liked, and the German soldier is puzzled why, despite the correctness of the Wehrmacht, he is so coldly received. He wants to have an explanation which blames someone outside the Army for this failure of the "New Order."

(V) *Respect for Western Powers.* The German has a sense of inferiority to both Britain and America. Many Nazis, for instance, regard National Socialism as the method of making Germany a ruling race "like the British." The German feelings for Britain are a confused mixture of envy, respect and contempt for the old-fashioned. Their feeling for America is different, since they do not feel to it a racial unity like Britain or Germany, and are suspicious of its "capitalist imperialism." They profoundly respect its riches, production capacity and "smartness", and regard it as the continent of unlimited possibilities.

Intensive propaganda has failed to modify these traditional feelings. *In particular nearly all German soldiers are confident that they will be treated well as prisoners of war and hope for (if they do not expect) an Anglo-American occupation if the worst comes to the worst.* Furthermore, they are feverishly anxious for Anglo-American appreciation of "the chivalry" of the Wehrmacht.

(VI) *The Shadow of the Two Front War.* It is improbable that German fighting morale in the West will be seriously undermined before a successful Anglo-American landing, provided there is no great German disaster in the East. But the moment we can announce a decisive breakthrough will be a moment of profound psychological crisis, greater even than the shock of Mussolini's collapse last year.

Meanwhile, the advance of the Russian troops *into Europe* must reduce the persuasiveness of the argument that Hitler is deliberately yielding space in the East to ensure victory in the West. Gradually the German soldier begins to ask whether Hitler's strategy is not precisely what United Nations strategy desires, and whether the Second Front is not having its effects even before it starts.

The Strategy of Psychological Warfare

14. The foregoing analysis suggests that, provided there is no catastrophe in the East, the weak points in German morale, enumerated above, will begin to counteract the strong points only when the Anglo-American forces have demonstrated that they can use their quantitative superiority.

15. It is impossible to predict at what phase of the operations this change in German morale will come. On this point Psychological Warfare will be guided by G-2. Already, however, it is possible to lay down two phases in the psychological warfare campaign:
   (a) The phase before and after D-day up to change in German morale (referred to as *Phase A*).
   (b) The phase after the change (referred to as *Phase B*).
The present Directive deals with *Phase A*.

16. In Phase A all psychological warfare against German troops must be regarded as *preparatory*. This must be a period *not* of *direct assault* or of open appeals for surrender; but of steady repetition of the facts, full recognition of which will bear sudden fruit in Phase B.

Even after D-day this unemphatic reiteration of facts should be continued until evidence from G-2 indicates that it is time to move into Phase B.

17. During this phase psychological warfare will concentrate on the following tasks:
   (I) *Long-term tasks.*
      (a) Maintenance and increase of belief in the reliability of the Anglo-American word, and of unity between the Russians and ourselves.
      (b) Creation of an atmosphere in which the German soldier gradually comes to feel that, since defeat is certain, he has fulfilled his soldierly duty and can now follow the example of the German Army in Tunisia.
   (II) *Short-term tasks, pre D-day.*
      (a) Stimulation of defeatism through a sense of Anglo-American superiority in men and materials; combatting the fear of Bolshevism by a cautious build-up of Anglo-American strength.
      (b) Exploitation of German confidence in the good treatment of prisoners of war so as to decrease German fighting spirit and undermine German fear of defeat. Simultaneously, familiarisation of the German soldier with official Allied statements on the place of Germany in Post-War Europe.
      (c) Exploitation of the Russian offensive as exemplifying the certainty of a German defeat in a two front war.
      (d) Exploitation of the German fear of sabotage and resistance by occupied peoples, including foreign workers.
      (e) Exploitation of a sense of isolation through the Allied threat to German communications.
      (f) Exploitation of the air offensive to stimulate distrust between the air force and the army and to undermine confidence in the possibility of successful resistance.

(III) *Short-term tasks post D-Day.* After D-day the following tasks should be added to those in (II) above:
  (a) Stimulation of distrust of foreigners in the German army by open incitement of these foreigners.
  (b) Special attacks on the morale of troops on the flanks of the fighting. Since these troops will not be actually engaged, they will probably form the best target for propaganda. In this campaign emphasize the failure of the Luftwaffe and the German Navy to prevent the landings.

Methods to be employed in carrying out the above Campaign

18. Long—term tasks.

(I) *Maintenance and increase of belief in the reliability of the Anglo-American word and in unity between the Russians and ourselves.*

  (a) Throughout this phase all psychological warfare in all media, whether tactical or strategic, will remain factual and objective, avoiding terms, phrases, or pictures which the German soldier will dismiss as "propaganda." In particular, all boasting and sneering will be scrupulously avoided; there will be no direct appeals to the soldier's self-interest. There will be no attempts at a chummy or intimate style. All psychological warfare will give the impression of Anglo-American reliability, reticence, soldierly dignity and decency.
  (b) Use every opportunity to demonstrate practical collaboration between ourselves and the Russians. This is preferable to ideological dissertations on United Nations Unity.

(II) *Creation of an atmosphere in which the German soldier gradually comes to feel that, since defeat is certain, he has fulfilled his soldierly duty and can now follow the example of the German Army in Tunisia.*

Do not assume that the German soldier is yet convinced that defeat is certain. He is keyed-up and may maintain a relatively high morale for some time after D-day.

Concentrate therefore on those facts which the German soldier can accept as facts, illustrating the inevitability of ultimate defeat.

Make no open appeals for deserting. Similarly, make no open appeals to fear, e.g. of the air offensive. Treat the German soldier as a man who, if openly incited by the enemy to cowardice, will do the opposite.

Show the increasing isolation of Germany's position in the world and the gradual weakening and disintegration of the satellites, the increasing restrictions being imposed on Germany by the neutrals, and the defeats suffered by her Japanese allies.

19. Short-term tasks pre-D-day.

(I) *Stimulation of defeatism through a sense of Anglo-American superiority in men and materials; combatting the fear of Bolshevism by a cautious buildup of Anglo-American strength.*

Do not try to heighten the tension by a deliberate war of nerves campaign. The German will see through this and dismiss it as propaganda. But provide all material available, especially technical material, on the leadership, organisation, equipment, and training of the Anglo-American armies.

Continue to provide facts showing the failure of the U-boats.

Show that the Mediterranean fronts are draining away German reserves needed for the two essential fronts.

(II) *Exploitation of German confidence in the good treatment of prisoners of war so as to decrease German fighting spirit and undermine German fear of defeat. Simultaneously, familiarization of the German soldier with official Allied statements on the place of Germany in post-war Europe.*

Continue and increase the campaign illustrating the treatment of German prisoners of war. But avoid, especially in leaflets a "display" which looks like commercial publicity. In radio propaganda increase as far as possible broadcasts about, and by German prisoners of war.

It is probable that many German soldiers are not familiar with even the few statements available on United Nations intentions with regard to post-war Germany. These statements should now be plugged in leaflets and radio. Equally, the fact should be emphasised that the Nazis are deliberately concealing from the German soldier the real intentions of the United Nations.

(III) *Exploitation of the Russian offensive as exemplifying the certainty of a German defeat in a two-front war.*

Destroy the illusion that the German retreat in the East is deliberately planned by showing the intimate connection between Russian and Anglo-American strategy. Hitler is no longer the master of his own strategy. It is dictated to him by the two-front strategy of the United Nations.

Treat the Mediterranean as a theater in which we have compelled the Germans to fritter away first class manpower and reserves vitally needed for the decisive battles on the two major fronts.

(IV) *Exploitation of the German fear of sabotage and resistance by occupied peoples, including foreign workers.*

Never appeal directly to German fear of sabotage and resistance. Confine yourself to plain facts. Do not spoil these facts by headlines such as "Martyrs of Gestapo Terror."

Build up the impression that resistance in occupied Europe, and to a lesser extent in Germany, is an organised part of the Anglo-American strategy.

Stress where possible facts indicating the decline of effective police control in Germany and German-occupied Europe. Here again do not interpret these facts to the Germans, but let them speak for themselves. *Make no references before D-day to foreigners serving in the German Armies in the West.*

(V) *Exploitation of a sense of isolation through the Allied threat to German communications.*

Make the German soldier (espacially in the coastal divisions) feel he is a "human land mine", by stressing the significance of attacks on German communications.

Stress that the Atlantic Wall is 1000 miles long and that the German High Command can only meet a threat at one point by stripping reserves from other points. The German assumes that there will be several landings: so should we.

(VI) *Exploitation of the air offensive to stimulate distrust between the air force and the army and to undermine confidence in the possibility of successful resistance.*

"Fear propaganda" designed to intensify the effect of bombs has been rendered unnecessary by the bombs themselves. In treating the air offensive concentrate on its strictly military significance as an essential part of our invasion strategy. Avoid giving any impression that we are trying to break German morale. Seek indirectly to arouse resentment against the fact that air power, which the Nazis claimed as their invention, has now been turned against Germany. Give the impression that the efforts of the Luftwaffe cannot make up for Anglo-American production superiority and for the mistakes of the German leadership.

Remember that production figures—unrelated to battle figures—no longer impress the German soldier. Not the number of aircraft produced, but the effects of air superiority impress him. This applies also to all forms of manpower and material superfority.

16. Short-term tasks post D-day.

(I) *Stimulation of distrust of foreigners in the German army by open incitement of these foreigners.*

On and after D-day a special campaign will be launched of direct incitement to desertion addressed to foreigners in the German army of the West. It will have two objects: (I) to influence the foreigners, (II) indirectly to influence the German troops. A special directive will be issued on this subject.

(II) *Special attacks on the morale of troops on the flanks of the fighting.*

During the actual fighting we cannot expect that the German troops engaged will be receptive to anything but combat propaganda.

Strategic radio and leaflets should in this period be directed chiefly to the German troops on the flanks, as well as to foreigners throughout the German Army. The treatment should remain formal and objective and avoid boasting or creating an atmosphere of undue excitement. Every effort should be made to obtain "hot" statements from prisoners of war for use by radio and leaflet.

Every effort should be made to demonstrate to these troops the influence of sea power on the operation. In particular the following themes should be used:

(a) Allied command of the sea and of the air over it gives us the power to launch attacks with the maximum of surprise over a very wide range.

(b) Allied command of the sea excludes the free use of sea communications along the Atlantic Wall, communications which would be invaluable if land communications are destroyed or hampered.

(c) The German Navy cannot both cope with the assault and its follow up, and with the trans-atlantic traffic bringing more and more men, weapons and supplies.

(d) To the troops on the flanks of the breach in the Atlantic Wall, emphasise the power and effectiveness of naval bombardment.

(e) Complete Allied control of the Mediterranean offers freedom of action for further attacks on the Continent.

APPENDIX "E"

Psychological Warfare Operations against German Army Commanders to induce Surrender

(Recommendations to G-3 from PWD relative to development of techniques based on experience to date—November 3, 1944.)

Discussion

1. The issue of ultimata to German commanders to induce rapid surrender to the Allies has, in some instances, been effective, and, in others, has merely resulted in stiffened resistance. This Division has been called upon to undertake Psychological Warfare operations sometimes prior to delivery of the ultimatum and, invariably, after the ultimatum has been rejected. Experience in these operations tends to show that, if certain psychological factors inherent in the personal as well as the military situation of the German commander are taken into account prior to the issue of an ultimatum and if Psychological Warfare operations can be phased according to a deliberate plan, based partly on general and partly on tactical considerations, there is a greater likelihood of the ultimatum being accepted at an early stage. This paper discusses some of the principles involved, and proposes a procedure to be adopted by Army Groups and Armies in future similar operations.

General Principles

2. Psychological Warfare operations against beleaguered German forces or garrisons are of two distinct types:
   a. Operations directed against the German commander in person.
   b. Operations devised, directly or indirectly, against the main body of troops.

3. These two types often conflict with each other. Psychological Warfare leaflets and special radio broadcasts directed against the troops and designed to induce surrender or desertion invariably come to the attention of and influence the German commander and his staff officers. Any conciliatory action by the German commander which appears to be the direct result of propaganda pressure places him in an impossible position with his own staff. If it is remembered that only the commander himself can effect the surrender of the German force as a whole, it is also obvious that a leaflet which, for example, discloses to his troops confidential discussions of the commander with Allied representatives may well infuriate the former into ordering continuing resis-

tance, although it may simultaneously have an excellent effect in undermining the morale of the troops and accelerating desertions.

4. An important by-product of the two above-mentioned types of action, especially in the case of a completely surrounded garrison, is the effect produced by the surrender, or the continuation of the battle, on other German commanders and on the German public. Likewise, if German propaganda builds up the commander as an "epic" figure, as at Brest, this must be borne in mind in propaganda. The widespread Allied publicity given to the Aachen ultimatum probably had an adverse effect on the strictly tactical position. On the other hand, the strategic advantages of creating "a lesson of Aachen" probably outweighed the tactical disadvantages, although it would appear wiser not to attempt to create strategic propaganda effects from a local situation, but to concentrate exclusively on the tactical task.

Factors affecting German Commander's will to resist.

5. The German commander's desire to fight on or surrender is influenced by the following calculable factors:

   a. *Directive from his superiors.* In only one case so far, that of General ELSTER'S command south of the Loire (which by its nature, being amorphous and exposed, was not a surrounded garrison proper), did a commander surrender without even the appearance of resistance. In all other cases, at least the letter, if not always the spirit, of the order to resist was obeyed.

   b. *Military pressure.* In an extreme case, such as that of CONCARNEAU, the commander was in the end willing to surrender after token pressure had been applied. At CHERBOURG, after reduction of most of the port, token shelling by smoke shells produced the surrender of one junior German commander.

   c. *Staff officers.* Their quality and background is an important element. In at least one instance, surrender was decided upon after a round-table discussion. The general attitude of the staff, as well as that of the commander, is therefore important.

   d. *Threats against the commander's family.* This has of late become an increasingly important factor. Colonel WILCK (commander at AACHEN), prompted by fear of reprisals against his family, inserted in the surrender document a clause to the effect that the food and ammunition of his command were exhausted, in order to help justify his surrender.

   e *The tactical situation,* per se, and the tactical and supply situation as reported in the German home press. The surrender or desertion of small groups of German soldiers may sometimes influence the tactical situation, but, where this is the case, it does not greatly influence or exercise much moral pressure on the commander.

6. Extensive prisoner interrogation has established the fact that, in the view of the German soldier, "holding out to the last man" is an order which is not considered to the commander, or even to the residual force, in a tactically impossible situation. In no case was the ultimate surrender of the garrison thought dishonourable or contrary to the hold-out order. To hold-out to the last man in never held to apply to hopeless ("pistols against tanks") local situations such as prevailed in the last days of the CROZON Peninsula (BREST) campaign.

Action Prior to Issue of Ultimatum

7. It is essential that Psychological Warfare against the German commander and his troops be conducted in such a way that an early surrender will appear "honourable" to his troops, the home public and the home leadership. Thus, it is important that contact be made as soon as possible through parliamentaries with the commander, under conditions of secrecy and privacy, and especially without publicity, before the propaganda operation has gathered momentum. The object of the first discussion should not necessarily be to induce an immediate surrender, which in any event is unlikely, but to ascertain the degree of resistance which the commander intends to put up, and the extent to which he can be influenced by token actions of the Allies and by "a good press". The Agreements reached with Admiral SCHIRLITZ at LA PALLICE (La Rochelle) relative to non-destruction of the port provided there was no Allied air action are a good examples of a successful parley.

8. If no explicit or implicit arrangement for an early surrender is made at the first parley, nevertheless the subsequent propaganda directed to the troops should be essentially quiet in tone and informative in substance until the first major Allied attack has

taken place and gives the commander a new reason to discuss cessation of hostilities. If the first major attack achieves no remarkable tactical success, little can probably be gained by renewing contact with the German commander. On the other hand, a distinct tactical success, appropriately reported by Allied press and wireless, so as to emphasize the hopelessness of the German commander's position, would be a strong inducement to him to re-open negotiations.

Suggested Sequence of Procedure

9. The following procedure, both in negotiations and in the conduct of Psychological Warfare operations, is therefore suggested:—
   a. Every effort should be made at the earliest moment to establish and maintain some sort of contact, via parlementaires or agents, with the enemy commander, and utmost secrecy maintained.
   b. Firmness, determination, correctness, and lack of compromise must be shown in all dealings with the commander. But, to carry determination to the extent of issuing an ultimatum without an attempt at a parley is clearly unprofitable, and it is especially unprofitable to publicize its rejection, as this serves only to commit the commander to an uncompromising position. The fact that arbitrary ultimata are undesirable was clearly brought out in the BREST operation. The successful operations against LE HAVRE and BOULOGNE were conducted without ultimata. The AACHEN ultimatum was a long-range propaganda asset, but tactically unproductive. The German commander who is in a position to accept an ultimatum is more likely to arrange his surrender at a parley.
   c. It is likewise unprofitable to vilify the enemy commander, or even to give him special mention in propaganda. Experience with Colonel AULOCH (who commanded ST. MALO and was extensively interrogated later) showed that the publicity he received was a factor in prolonging his resistance; in fact, this commander believed that decorations, and his promotion to Major General, were the direct outcome of Allied publicity.
   d. Propaganda should not take the line that previous commanders surrendered after first proclaiming their will to resist to the end. This creates the impression that they surrendered earlier than necessary and so may deter future surrenders, since;
      (1) Neither the German commander nor his troops are willing to believe this. RAMCKE, AULOCH, etc. have very high prestige.
      (2) It creates a competing situation in which each commander tries to hold out longer than another.
      (3) It attaches a negative note to surrender, implying that we despise the Germans for surrendering after first proclaiming they would not.

Conclusions

10. It would appear, from the facts cited in paragraphs 2 to 8 inclusive, that a definite agreed technique could profitably be developed to induce quicker surrenders and so minimize expenditure of effort by Allied forces. Adoption of a definite procedure would entail the following action:—
    a. The steps leading up to and including the delivery of suggestions of surrender should be planned as specialised operations requiring expert information and advice. The local Commanders on the ground should be made aware of this, and a simple system for supplying the specialised information and advice should be instituted and all concerned informed.
    b. Army Groups should be informed of (a.) above for dissemination to lower commanders, and should be asked to direct them to call for the following specialised information and personnel, as required:
       (1) Detailed biographies, and other pertinent information, of the German commander and his senior staff officers which are available in Psychological Warfare Division records, so as to give an understanding of the commander's psychology and the best methods of approach for purposes of parley.
       (2) General information from Psychological Warfare Division as to the best methods of handling the commander, both before and during surrender negotiations, and in assuring that the propaganda carried on during the negotiations shall not jeopardise their success.
       (3) The attachment, for temporary duty, of Psychological Warfare Division officers having special knowledge and language qualifications.

APPENDIX "G"
Final Report on Leaflet Operation

(In part, this duplicates the chapter on Leaflets, in the main section of this account. However, it goes into far greater detail and contains samples of leaflets, and charts covering the operation.)

Leaflet Operations in the Western European Theater
(Prepared by Maj. Robert H. Garet, AC)

1. SUMMARY

A total of approximately 5,997,000,000 leaflet units was distributed over the Continent by aircraft based in the United Kingdom during the leaflet operation in the Western European Theater, which continued on an increasing scale until the unconditional surrender of Germany in May 1945. During this time, the objectives and methods of this leaflet distribution underwent considerable changes in order to keep pace with the developments of the war.

In the pre-D-Day period, 2,750,000,000 leaflets were distributed; 2,151,000,000 by the Royal Air Force and 599,000,000 by the Eighth Air Force, which started leaflet operations in August 1943. In the early phases, these leaflets were almost entirely of a long-range political nature. After the Germans occupied most of Western Europe and the maintenance of morale and the spirit of resistance in these countries became of paramount importance, a large proportion of the leaflets were aimed at the inhabitants of these occupied countries.

With the Allied landings on D-Day, the leaflet campaign became a closely integrated part of the military operations. From D-Day on, although the Army Group and Army Psychological Warfare Units in the field produced substantial quantities of leaflets for local distribution by fighter bombers and artillery, the great bulk of the leaflets (approximately 90%) were produced by PWD-SHAEF, and distributed by aircraft based in the United Kingdom. For the most part, they fell into two categories: tactical leaflets aimed at reducing the enemy's combat strength by impairing morale and persuading the individual soldier to stop fighting, and strategic leaflets, designed to make civilians take action favorable to the Allied military operations. During this period, a total of 3,240,000,000 leaflets were distributed; 405,000,000 by the Royal Air Force, 1,577,000,000 by the Special Leaflet Squadron, 1,176,000,000 by the Eighth Air Force on daylight bombing missions and 82,000,000 on special leaflet missions by medium bombers of the Allied Expeditionary Air Forces before they moved to the Continent.

2. ORGANIZATION AND FUNCTIONS

1. The organizations charged with the responsibility for overt psychological warfare in the Western European Theater, which included as one of its major operations the distribution of "white" leaflets, were the Office of War Information (representing the US State Department), the Political Intelligence Department (representing the British Foreign Office) and the Psychological Warfare Division of SHAEF (representing the Supreme Commander).

2. Subversive or "black" propaganda was a separate operation which was the joint responsibility of PID and the Office of Strategic Services (representing the US. War Department). This operation is only briefly covered in this report as it was not a PWD responsibility, although the Leaflet Section participated in the distribution of "black" propaganda.

3. The civilian agencies were responsible for the political aspects of propanganda, and PWD for the military, but as there was no clear dividing line between the two, close coordination was necessary between the three organizations. This was accomplished at a high level by the Tri-Partite Comittee (composed of the chiefs of the three organizations) and by direct liaison between the operational sections involved. (See Exhibit 1.)

4. Before D-Day, all leaflets were produced by the civilian agencies, but after D-Day, PWD produced the great bulk of the leaflets, with the civilian agencies acting in an advisory capacity and producing only a few leaflets of a purley political character. (See Exhibit 2.) An exception was the newspaper "Nachrichten," which was produced for PWD by a special PID-OSS editorial team.

5. To handle the detailed mechanics of production and distribution during the

SHAEF period, there were in effect four echelons, each with its own special aptitude for performing a particular task:

a. *The Civilian Agencies (OWI, PID, OSS).* These were equipped with complete news-gathering facilities, trained writing personnel, typographical and printing plants, as well as art and layout personnel. Their writing facilities were available for newssheets and periodicals addressed to civilians of enemy occupied countries and for special strategic leaflets addressed to enemy civilians. Furthermore, the special news-gathering facilities available to PID and OSS made them the logical group to edit "Nachrichten" the daily "gray" newspaper in German—originally designed exclusively for drop on German troops, and later, distributed to German civilians as well. A Joint Production Unit was established by these agencies to handle all leaflets printed in the United Kingdom.

b. *PWD-SHAEF (the Psychological Warfare Division, Supreme Headquarters, Allied Expeditionary Force).* This special section of General Eisenhower's staff was set up to handle all the psychological warfare activities of SHAEF. It worked in close coordination with the other staff sections, particularly G-2, G-3 and G-5, and thus was able to plan psychological warfare campaigns as an integral part of the military operation.

The Leaflet Section of PWD-SHAEF, which included its own writing team and controlled a special leaflet squadron of heavy bombers, and a packing and trucking unit for servicing British-based aircraft with leaflet bombs, was charged with the following functions:

(1) Policy guidance of and coordination with the leaflet units at the Army Group level.
(2) The production of general tactical and strategic leaflets, with the exception of a few special strategic leaflets on political themes produced by the civilian agencies.
(3) The distribution of all general tactical leaflets from the United Kingdom, and jointly with PID., the distribution of all strategic leaflets.
(4) The production and delivery to the Army Groups of such SHAEF leaflets as they required for their own distribution.
(5) The preparation and distribution of reaction reports and similar material designed to facilitate and expand the leaflet operation by explaining its nature and emphasizing its importance.
(6) Liaison with the Air Forces. Production or procurement of leaflet bombs and other material, pick-ups, packing into bombs, and delivery of all leaflets to the airfields.
(7) Coordination with the Joint Production Unit.

In actual practice, the Leaflet Section assumed an even larger proportion of the total Allied leafleting effort than had been originally planned. Its Special Leafleting Squadron was the only air force unit under the operational control of PWD, and therefore, the only one available at all times for distribution where and when it was most needed. In addition, production and trucking facilities in the United Kingdom were vastly superior to those on the Continent. As a result, the great bulk (roughly 90%) of all air-dropped leaflets, both tactical and strategic, were produced in the United Kingdom and distributed by United Kingdom-based heavy bombers.

c. *The Psychological Warfare Units of the Army Groups.* Leaflet functions at Army Groups varied according to the equipment and personnel available to the Army Group and Army teams respectively. Two other factors conditioned Army Group leaflet activities: first, overall propaganda lines were determined at the SHAEF level, and second, the Army teams because of their forward locations and better tactical intelligence, were the ideal agencies for the output of purely tactical propaganda. To the Army Group Units remained several vital functions in the overall leaflet effort:

(1) Production of semi-tactical newssheets and general tactical leaflets for situations applying uniquely along their own Army Group fronts.
(2) Air liaison, including coordination of fighter-bomber drops by tactical air commands, passing of target requests for the Special Leaflet Squadron from Army teams to SHAEF, and, in the case of the Twelfth Army Group, direction of medium bomber drops.
(3) Intelligence. The Intelligence Section of the Twelfth Army Group Psychological Warfare Unit gathered considerable leaflet reaction material and consolidated leaflet intelligence material from the Army teams. Although much of the work of this section was not concerned solely with the leaflets, but with the psychological warfare effort as a whole, it was of value to those concerned with leaflet production and distribution at all echelons.

(4) The procurement of SHAEF leaflets, printed in the United Kingdom, for artillery dissemination by Armies.

Staff position. In the Twelfth and Twenty-first Army Groups psychological warfare was organized as one of the dual functions of the Publicity and Psychological Warfare (P. and PW.) Section, a separate staff section responsible to the Chief of Staff. At Sixth Army Group Headquarters, psychological warfare became a sub-section of G-2, giving it the advantages of access to G-2s extensive intelligence-gathering facilities.

Difference in function and organization at various Army Groups. At the Twenty-first Army Group, limited printing facilities at Army level necessitated production of a considerable number of tactical leaflets at group, but limited personnel prevented any extensive psychological warfare intelligence activities. In the Twelfth Army Group, the Army teams usually had adequate printing facilities available, and the Army Group produced less than a dozen different leaflets almost entirely of a general tactical nature, in addition to the newssheets "Frontpost" and "Feldpost". At the Sixth Army Group, the dual French-American nature of the command, and the smaller psychological warfare section, made liaison the principal function at group level, and the newssheet "Frontbrief", as well as all leaflets, were put out by the Army teams.

d. *The Army Psychological Warfare Teams*, which were best able, because of their forward location and rapid intelligence to exploit local tactical situations with combat leaflets aimed at specific enemy units and positions. Much of the effectiveness of the Army team derives from its unique ability to produce and distribute these leaflets quickly and, above all, to direct coordinated loudspeaker and leaflet missions at the request of local commanders.

These teams, which functioned either under G-2 or as separate units, were considerably hampered by initial shortages of personnel and equipment. Often improvising in the field, printing on mobile equipment and in local plants where these were available, some Army teams were responsible in the closing days of the campaign for the dissemination by artillery shell and fighter bomber of a million or more leaflets daily.

In addition to the output of local tactical combat leaflets, Army psychological warfare units performed several other leaflet functions, roughly paralleling those at Army Group:

(1) Output of a limited number of general tactical leaflets, and in the case of the Seventh Army, a weekly newssheet.
(2) Air liaison, involving coordination of requests from divisions and corps for leaflet drops by fighter bombers and the SHAEF Special Squadron.
(3) Artillery liaison, including filling of requests by lower echelons for artillery leaflets, procuring SHAEF leaflets for artillery use, assuring the supply of propaganda shells and the loading and transport of these shells to firing points.
(4) Intelligence. Army combat loudspeaker teams in the front lines and interrogators at POW cages provided vital information for use in propaganda operations at all levels.

e. *Coordination between echelons. (See Exhibit 3.)*
(1) Between SHAEF and the civilian agencies. After D-Day, as the leaflet operation became more tactical, SHAEF produced a larger percentage of the leaflets and the civilian agencies limited themselves to a general policy supervision except in cases where political issues were involved when it was necessary for the leaflets and radio to be closely coordinated. (See Exhibit 2.) They continued, however, to edit "Nachrichten" which became more and more important, and in the closing months of the campaign accounted for about 60% of the available air lift.
(2) Between SHAEF and the Army Groups.

Note: Although the pattern of coordination between SHAEF and each of the Army Groups was basically the same, the remarks below apply to coordination with the Twelfth Army Group to a much larger extent than to the other Army Groups.

(a) Directives were issued at irregular intervals, covering important strategic developments—such as the Rundstedt counter-offensive, the crossing of the Rhine—or important general topics—such as the treatment of Military Government by our propaganda. Such directives were prepared by PWD and issued by SHAEF under the authority of the Chief of Staff.
(b) Periodic written guidances, daily (by cable) and weekly, which were used to clarify policy points which came up in the preceding period, and which were passed down to armies by the Army Groups. Guidances were usually found to cover topics too limited in time to be of use for tactical leaflet writers, but were useful for policy control of the newsheets.

(c) Periodic meetings, usually on a fortnightly basis, during which tactical leaflet problems were discussed. Such questions as how to meet the German "Victory or Siberia" line, were first discussed at the fortnightly meeting, later, formulated and disposed of in a weekly guidance.

(d) Overall leaflet directives. A basic psychological warfare directive was issued by SHAEF before the invasion, mainly containing a basic appreciation of German soldier morale. One other, considerably shorter and more precise directive was produced later in the campaign, chiefly in order to assure a maximum of similarity in the various approaches, and to avoid fundamental blunders to which Army teams under pressure from field commands were likely to be subject.

(e) Perhaps the most important method of coordination lay in the exchange of leaflets and intelligence between the Armies, Army Groups and SHAEF.

(f) Informal correspondence between the leaflet writers on the various echelons were helpful to achieve some coordination. At irregular intervals, SHAEF also issued letters cataloguing current strategic leaflets, outlining their objectives and discussing the policy behind them.

(g) Flow of intelligence. An important element in the coordination of leaflet policy between the various echelons was the continuous flow of German soldier and civilian intelligence to SHAEF from the Armies and Army Groups, as well as from its own intelligence officers in the field. Interrogations by the forward teams not only furnished output material for the leaflet newspapers and newssheets, but also turned up important new trends in German morale and in German soldier psychology (e.g., the "Victory or Siberia" theme), which often were the subject of further, more detailed interrogations and quantitative analyses by polls.

This large body of intelligence was the underlying basis of guidances and directives and the agenda of meetings between representatives of various echelons. Moreover, aside from outright policy directives or guidances based on the intelligence available at SHAEF, the lower echelons had the benefit of receiving evaluated material consisting of consolidated evidence from several sources, and the results of studies (such as prisoner polls on the popularity of Hitler) which helped them in their understanding and implementation of the agreed policy.

(3) Between SHAEF and the Army teams. Personal contact by visits between the German output personnel of SHAEF and the Armies—with permission of the Army Groups in every case—enabled many of the policy problems to be discussed on the spot, and valuable guidance to be furnished in this manner, in addition to the coordination through the Army Groups. As the Army teams frequently had to produce leaflets under directive from their Army commander or on request from forward units, local tactical propaganda was far less coordinated than general tactical (i.e., more long-term) leaflets produced by the Army teams.

3. MEDIA AND POLICY
1. The Leaflet Media

News was found, early in the campaign, to be the most effective means to undermine the enemy's morale and to secure the necessary attention for the basic surrender message to the enemy. Aside from news leaflets (see b. (1) below), the following publications were disseminated to the enemy:—

a. *Leaflet Newspapers.*

(1) "N a c h r i c h t e n   f ü r   d i e   T r u p p e" was a daily leaflet newspaper, at first of two, and then of four sides, which was dropped continuously on or behind the German Western front from before D-Day (25 April 1944) until the German capitulation. It was a political warfare venture planned especially for operation "OVERLORD" by a joint British and American staff from PID and OSS owing to the fact that it was produced in England, in close touch with the Headquarters of the Supreme Commander, it had certain unique features which distinguish it from other successful newspapers dropped on German troops in other theaters.

It combined accurate, up-to-the-minute military news gained from all possible sources with international and German home news from the many sources of information, some of them secret, available to PID and OSS. Depending for its appeal on this complete news coverage, otherwise unavailable to German troops, it relied for its effectiveness on indirect propaganda aimed at undermining the German's faith in his leaders and convincing him of the inevitability of defeat. Originally designed to be a purely tactical newspaper, it was later used on civilian targets as well.

The project of such a daily newspaper would have been impossible without the virtual guarantee of daily distribution given by the Special Squadron of the Eighth Air Force. Weather conditions frequently interrupted continuous delivery, but during the height of the Normandy battle, important railway and road junctions and key towns behind the German lines must have received their "Nachrichten" in large quantities as regularly as their breakfasts. A number of special drops were also arranged on cut-off garrisons, e.g. Cherbourg, Le Havre, the Ardennes pocket, Holland, in which the whole emphasis on the front news was on the particular tactical situation of the troops on whom the newspaper was dropped.

The newspaper was normally written and made up between 2200 hours of one day and 0600 hours of the next. It would then be dropped 18 to 24 hours later, although daylight drops have taken place at even shorter intervals. When big Allied operations were impending it was necessary to ensure that the newspaper dropped on the night of D-Day should contain at least headlines and an outline story of what had happened the same morning. For example, on the day of the Normandy landings, several hundred thousand newspapers announcing the breach of the Atlantic Wall in several places were dropped on German reserve divisions in Normandy the same night. This would have been impossible without that close cooperation and confidence which existed between editors of the newspaper, the senior officers of PWD-SHAEF and the intelligence and operational staffs of the Supreme Commander.

The daily production of "Nachrichten" proceeded without interruption from 25 April 1944 to 4 May 1945, when the final issue announced the end of hostilities in the West. Ten to twelve thousand words were written, sub-edited and headlined daily; news photographs were secured and reproduced nightly through a special service of cars from London to the country headquarters of PID; up to half a million copies daily—sometimes more—were distributed to airdromes, packed in bombs and delivered to general and pinpoint targets selected in daily conferences between military and PWD staffs. The newspaper employed the services of roughly 25 editorial, and between 70 and 80 printers and distribution staff.

(2) "Frontpost" was a weekly, semi-tactical newspaper produced by the Twelfth Army Group for dissemination by fighter bomber and medium bomber. This paper was especially angled for the requirements of the particular Army Group front, and being a „white" publication, stressed the surrender angle more in the nature of a combat leaflet. Produced in the field, and without the benefit of the extensive civilian organization available in the United Kingdom, "Frontpost" was a "semihot" medium, usually slightly less timely than "Nachrichten." An abridged version, "Feldpost," was furnished to lower echelons for additional artillery dissemination.

(3) "Frontbrief" was a weekly newspaper published by the Seventh US Army team under field conditions. Especially during the winter when that Army proved difficult to service by the Special Leaflet Squadron due to its distance from base (a factor especially during bad weather), "Frontbrief" proved to be virtually the only news source for Germans in that sector. As a timely publication, it lagged somewhat behind either "Nachrichten" or "Frontpost".

b. *General Tactical Leaflets.*

This kind of leaflet, which was usually produced by PWD-SHAEF and disseminated by the Special Leaflet Squadron from the United Kingdom, included appeals to the German soldier, usually dealt with the general surrender theme, as distinguished from leaflets written for particular units in locally limited situations. The need for dissemination of general surrender leaflets in great bulk by bomber was demonstrated in the campaign. Whereas artillery could pinpoint small targets more accurately, the dropping of leaflets along the enemy's line of retreat, before and during the mobile phase, could only be accomplished by bomber dissemination. General tactical leaflets can be divided into two classes:

(1) Static situations. During these periods, general tactical leaflets waged a war of attrition, dealing with general topics—either with news in its largest strategic sense (for instance, the July 1944 "putsch")—or exclusively with

the surrender theme, the treatment of prisoners, and the prospects of the individual reader in the battles to come. By far the largest portion of the output was taken up by this kind of general surrender propaganda, with clearly documented success.

(2) **Mobile situations.** Only the broadest aspects of the developing strategy could be exploited by general tactical leaflets, due to the fact that usually several day were taken up in their production. However, due to close liaison with the Army Groups, the SHAEF-produced leaflets were able to exploit the chief tactical developments of the campaign in well-coordinated leaflet series—such as the landing, the Avranches breakthrough, the Falaise battle, the first assault on the Westwall, the Rundstedt counter-offensive, and finally, the crossing of the Rhine. The surrender theme was kept foremost in all of these situations.

c. *Local Tactical Leaflets.*

This includes leaflets written for a temporary situation occasioned by the battle, which is exploited by a short-lived, and therefore, necessarily quickly-produced leaflet. The ideal small-scale tactical medium is the Army team-produced and artillery—or fighter bomber—disseminated leaflet. The Army Groups and SHAEF were confined either to the treatment of big events (see b. (2) abve) or to the production (by SHAEF) of a line of "contingency" leaflets, such as "You are Surrounded", which were then available for heavy bomber drop upon call by forward units.

d. *Strategic Leaflets.*

These were entirely handled from the rear where the necessary large production facilities existed, and disseminated by heavy bombers—except for a small quantity of fighter bomber-disseminated Army leaflets addressed to specific German communities in the final phase. Three chief classifications of strategic leaflets are in order:

(1) **"General" (attrition) leaflets.** These leaflets were designed to undermine confidence in the regime and in the outcome of the war. As soon as the Allied entered Germany, instruction-type leaflets demanded higher priorities and these leaflets faded out of the picture.

(2) **Civilian instruction leaflets.** These consisted of warnings to specified communities, evacuation orders, instructions on how to save a town by surrender, on evasion of the Volkssturm, etc. They were exclusively produced by SHAEF and disseminated by heavy bombers.

(3) **Foreign worker leaflets.** Produced by SHAEF and distributed by heavy bombers from the United Kingdom, these leaflets pursued the double purpose of waging psychological warfare against the German authorities, and of issuing practical instructions to the widely dispersed foreign worker elements in Germany.

e. *Official Instruction Leaflets.*

Owing to the fact that these leaflets, in their character as documents, committed the Supreme Commander and the Allied Governments, they were exclusively produced by SHAEF and cleared by the Chief of Staff, usually in close cooperation with the civilian agencies who provided the radio outlet for such statements. Many of the civilian instruction leaflets and those addressed to foreign workers come under this classification. The most important document of this sort, however, was the official SHAEF. "Safe Conduct", which was signed by the Supreme Commander and guaranteed good treatment to German soldiers under the provisions of the Geneva Convention. Others were the official instructions to foreign workers, and the instructions to specified occupational groups, such as to railroad workers.

f. *"Black" Leaflets.*

These leaflets, which purported to originate from enemy sources, were the joint responsibility of PID and OSS (see 11. 2.). This was a special secret operation and cannot be discussed in detail in this report. Substantial quantities of this material were distributed by packing approximately five percent of them into the leaflet bombs along with Nachrichten, and it is believed to have been a very effective form of propaganda.

2. Leaflet Policy.

a. *Daily "gray" newspaper, „Nachrichten für die Truppe".*

An essential part of the "Nachrichten" operation was to provide German troops with an up-to-date and detailed account of events on the German home front, about which they heard nothing—or at best, only half truths—on the official German radio or in the official newsheets issued to them by trained propaganda teams. The sources of intelligence for such detailed treatment of the frictions, inequalities and gradual weakening of the German home front were in London, and with them, the small group of specialists able to provide that documentation and appreciation of German internal events which was required.

It was, of course, difficult in time of war to ensure complete accuracy for, and to give authenticity to, news of what was happening in Germany behind the German soldier's back. On the other hand, it was possible through special intelligence and advice received from military headquarters, both forward and in England, to secure reliable and fast news of happenings on the battlefield. It was, therefore, possible, as it were, to carry uncheckable irrefutable and highly subversive home news on the shoulders of checkable and topical front news. On many occasions, "Nachrichten" was able to give the German soldier his first news of notable military events such as the Allied landing in the south of France or the Arnhem landing. It, therefore, seems to have acquired a reputation for reliability in its war news which, it is reasonable to assume, many readers transferred unconsciously to its home news. It also carried news from the DNB service, which by presenting the reader with matter he could hear from official German sources gave the sheet an air of objective reporting.

The newspaper also included daily a leading article in a direct and personal style, addressed to the "comrades"—both officers and men—at the front in which the case against the Party, against the useless prolongation of the war, against the muddles and corruptions in the official hierarchy and against the destruction of German and European values by the National Socialists was directly attacked.

In detail, the newspaper was made up as follows: on the front page, and in some columns on the back page, the German soldier found the news story from each front on which German troops were fighting, his own Western Front being covered in great detail. These stories were so written as to encourage the German soldier in the West to look back over his shoulder. For example, it was continually emphasized before and during the Normandy campaign that the Russian front was the only one taken seriously by the Party and the High Command, and the front was represented as an example of useless sacrifice and diversion of strength. On page two, was the daily topical commentary by Lt. von O., expressing a critical, browned-off indignant attitude to the conduct of the war, both at home and at the front, and giving plausible and rational form to the soldiers' suppressed desires to slacken off and give up hope. On page three, the German soldier found startling and worrying news from home, suggesting the flagrant inequality in the sacrifices made by the man at the front and the leader at home, by the ordinary civilian and by the Party member. He learned about the scandals of reserved occupations, of the overworking of women, of conditions in children's evacuation camps, of "black marketing" in high quarters and of insincere and bombastic appeals for sacrifice by bosses and by wire-pullers hundreds of miles behind the front.

In addition, an attempt was made to keep before the German reader a picture of the world political situation and Germany's place in it in which particular attention was paid to the failures of Germany's satellites and allies. Sport news and pictures of pin-up girls assured that this page did not have a purely propaganda content, but plenty of reader interest and entertainment.

It is to be emphasized that this newspaper was in no sense official; the news it gave and the views it expressed daily were submitted neither to military censorship nor to policy approval. Security considerations were discussed by liaison officers in military headquarters and the main lines of policy were regularly discussed with PWD-SHAEF and the civilian agencies. It was, therefore, possible on occasions for campaigns to be conducted against the morale of German troops, which contained information and ideas with which it was not desired directly to associate the Supreme Commander and the Allied Governments. For example, the rumor was successfully spread that German airmen wishing to desert to Allied airfields would not be fired upon by ground defences if certain signals were given. Such signals were, in fact, never officially approved on the Allied side, but German pilots followed the instructions and landed safely none the less. Likewise, items of intelligence about German order of battle and possible intentions during such critical battles as Falaise, the Ardennes and the crossing of the Rhine, could be made use of in this unofficial newspaper because German intelligence knew quite well that tactical deception might be one of the newspaper's functions, and that it was, therefore, a dangerous guide to Allied estimates of any tactical situation.

"Nachrichten für die Truppe" was, therefore, able to combine the functions of a political leaflet, a strategic leaflet and sometimes, of a tactical leaflet. Its principle difference from other Allied tactical leaflets was that it was neither in style nor in approach, avowedly an Allied product. The German soldier knew quite well that it came from the Allies, but its writers took every trouble to avoid reminding him of the fact.

b. *Combat Leaflets.*

Since the topics of the day, including news from Germany, were treated by the daily leaflet newspaper, the soldier leaflets confined themselves to surrender propaganda, which was treated through general tactical leaflets (see 1. b. (1) and (2) above), official instruction leaflets and local tactical leaflets. The basic policy considerations underlying the use of these leaflets were as follows:

(1) C a p t i v i t y. All soldier leaflets dealt, in one form or another, incidentally or as a main theme, with the topic of capitivity. As all combat leaflets had as their objective the taking of prisoners, the theme of captivity was constantly kept before the mind of the German soldier.

(2) G o o d T r e a t m e n t. Perhaps the most impressive argument for the continued use of the good treatment theme was the fact that German soldiers, not trusting us to treat them well, kept our "safe conducts" on their person in great numbers, and that of many leaflets, they often tended to remember only the feature dealing with good treatment. As a cardinal theme, therefore, but treated with conservatism ("underplayed"), the good-treatment theme ran through the entire output.

(3) D e s e r t i o n v s. S u r r e n d e r. It was found that soldierly pride and feeling that desertion was dishonorable, were perhaps the most basic and unchanging factors of German soldier mentality, even among deserters. SHAEF, therefore, attempted to enforce a policy which pictured captivity entirely as something that "happened" to a German soldier—especially since detailed inquiries showed that the line between surrender and capture was indeed a thin one. It was found that such a distinction had no noticeable effect on the volume of desertions, while avoiding the danger of alienating the German readers who rejected the idea of desertion although quite willing to stretch a point when it came to getting captured. The uniform application of this policy, however, proved impossible due to considerable pressure on the forward teams whenever front-line commanders found themselves confronted with especially low-morale Germans units. Toward the end of the campaign, the policy was superseded by the use of the "Surrender Order". (See 2.d. (2) below).

(4) M a t e r i a l S u p e r i o r i t y. It has been deliberate policy to furnish the German soldier with a sop to his honor by continuously pointing out that however great his bravery, he was confronted by a crushing superiority of war material against which his soldierly qualities were useless. This simple line, whose effect was constantly checked by detailed prisoner interrogations, was basic to the SHAEF leaflets. The leaflets of Army teams, where more detailed information on specific units was available, tended more to stress specific deficiencies of German units. The effect obtained by this latter line was to disconcert the enemy by the extent of our knowledge.

(5) G e n e v a C o n v e n t i o n. Our adherence to the Convention, and the strict observation of its provisions in Canada and the United States, proved to be a great asset and was exploited throughout the campaign. Insistance on our observation of Article 75 of the Convention was an especially useful weapon in countering German claims that prisoners would be shipped to Russia.

(6) C a p i t u l a t i o n T h e m e. The Nazis' exploitation of our unconditional entire output.
of which was the projection of General Eisenhower as Military Governor, and the description of his regime as firm, but just. Capitulation as such was likewise shown to be a military act with many precedents, never—if on a tactical level—robbing the surrendering German soldier of his privileges under the Geneva Convention.

(7) E x c l u d e d T o p i c s. As the operation progressed and more and more intelligence on the German soldier accumulated, it became clear that a number of obvious propaganda arguments were either ineffective or could not be used for policy reasons. A useful view of the scope of combat propaganda and its progressive limitation to the above simple and basic points can be obtained from a consideration of the following excluded subjects:

(a) Outright revolutionary propaganda. The evidence clearly showed that there was little inclination on the part of either German soldiers or civilians to revolt, and that in any case, they both were under too much restraint to make this line of propaganda even remotely effective.

(b) Personal attacks on Hitler. The mystical and fanatical attachment to Hitler was found to have no direct connection with either the belief in victory or the willingness to surrender, and inasmuch as the objective was not to convert the soldier, but to get him so surrender, this subject was by-passed as a strong point of German morale.

(c) Divisions and splits, between Army and Party, and between officers and men, or between Army and SS, were found to be obtainable chiefly by indirection. The leaflet newspaper, "Nachrichten", giving news items permitting of invidious comparisons, or of suspicions of disloyalty or favoritism, was found to be the best means for accomplishing this purpose.

(d) Ideological warfare. Reeducation of the German soldier was conceived of as a post-hostilities problem. As more and more lost faith in victory, they likewise became ripe for new ideas. In that final stage, however, the unconditional surrender propaganda made it necessary to concentrate on the futility of fighting on, rather than on the promises offered by the democratic way of life. We were not offering democracy to Germany, but Military Government.

(e) Appeals by German generals. For reasons of high policy, we were unable to utilize the German general staff, whom we were pledged to render impotent, or our purposes—despite the fact that many German generals in Allied hands would have been willing to recommend surrender. Use was made, however, of the statements made by the German generals in Russian hands.

(f) Counter-propaganda. German claims or Nazi propaganda lies were never recognized or directly contradicted. It was believed the most effective method of handling them was either to ignore them entirely or to negate them with a positive line of propaganda.

In addition to sub-paragraph (d) above, it should be remembered that a number of topics associated with daily news, were covered by the daily newspaper „Nachrichten" and, therefore, omitted from the combat leaflet output. Among such topics were items exploiting the soldiers' anxiety about bombing, or about foreign workers in Germany, news about other fronts, secret weapons, etc. Furthermore, "black" propaganda dealt with such subjects as malingering, subversion and the aiding and abetting of desertion.

c. *Civilian Leaflets*

(1) Action Themes. Intelligence from German soldiers, and later from civilians in occupied Germany, showed that defeatism was so widespread and that the acceptance of Nazism was so complete and so efficiently enforced by terror, that many of our "attrition-type" leaflets met with the answer "You are right, but what can we do?". The problem therefore, was to find things the Germans could do to speed the end of the war without immediately risking their lives. Incitements to revolution were not used except in the final collapse situation, when they took the form of recommending steps to effect the surrender of towns or villages. The principal themes were as follows:

(a) Anti-evacuation theme (before we reached the Rhine).
(b) Evacuation of specified areas, designed as "danger areas."
(c) Anti-Volkssturm campaign (evasion of service, and surrender).
(d) Slow-down campaign, combined with the evacuation theme.
(e) Talk-to-the-soldier campaign (tied in with surrender theme).
(f) Avoid the needless destruction of your town (by surrender).

(2) Projection of Military Government, and of the authority of General Eisenhower. This closely tied in with the imposition of Allied authority on Germans, as used by "Voice of SHAEF" broadcasts, and capitalized on General Eisenhower's character and personality, as contrasted to that of Himmler. As in combat leaflets, no direct attack was made on Hitler. Rather, the National Socialist "terror system" and particularly, its foremost representative, Himmler, were held up as the alternatives to Military Government.

d. *Official Instruction Leaflets.*

Due to the prestige which such leaflets were intended to carry, committing as they did, the Allied Governments and the Supreme Commander personally, especial care was taken in their production—in the selection of type, layout, reproduction of insignia and in their printing. While the policy involved in the contents of such leaflets naturally was different in each case, two examples in the line of combat propaganda were of especial importance:—

(1) "The Safe Conduct." Designed as a document complete with the crests of Great Britain and the United States, the SHAEF insignia and the signature of the Supreme Commander, this leaflet embodied the relevant provisions of the Geneva Convention and instructed the Allied outposts to take the bearer prisoner and

treat him decently. So successful was this leaflet all through the campaign that it was mixed in the proportion of ten percent, and later, fifteen percent, with all other combat leaflets dropped. In situations especially favorable from a tactical point of view, bombs filled with nothing but "Safe Conducts" were dropped on German troops.

(2) The "Surrender Order." As defeatism spread through the German Army, it became more and more obvious that reasons for surrendering and general exhortations were insufficient to overcome the strong obedience to orders which prevented many German soldiers from ceasing resistance. Consequently, an order was designed which tried to substitute the authority of General Eisenhower for that of the German's own immediate superior, and to pit his prestige against that of his German counterparts. Instructions were given by SHAEF to use this order only in acute tactical situations where there were good chances that German soldiers would use it as an alibi for surrender.

e. *"Black" Leaflets.*

Purporting to come from enemy sources, these leaflets attempted to accomplish their aims by sublety and indirection. They covered a multitude of themes, and in general, were designed to weaken the enemy's morale by undermining the soldiers' confidence in the Nazi Party and the High Command. There were also special leaflets, such as forged German food and clothing coupons, travel orders, etc., which were intended to add to the enemy's administrative difficulties and provide additional work for the SS and the Gestapo.

4. PRODUCTION

1. SHAEF-Civilian Agencies Level

Functioning at this level was a Joint Production Unit maned by PID and OWI personnel. To work with this production unit, the PWD. Leaflet Section maintained a sub-office in the same building through which were channeled all copy to be printed, as well as the final proofs to be filed and copies of the leaflets to be distributed to the interested departments throughout the psychological warfare operation.

a. *Paper and printing* were the responsibility of the Joint Production Unit. Paper was requisitioned as needed from a joint Anglo-American pool administered by HM Stationery Office. To provide for these needs, approximately 1,000 tons of paper allocated for leaflets and periodicals (roughly half of it of British manufacture, and the other half shipped over from America) was fed into the joint pool per month.

All typesetting, except for small occasional overflows, was handled by a special typograph department of the Joint Production Unit. From this department the completed forms were sent out for plate-making and printing to regular commercial houses under contract to the unit.

From D-Day through April 1945, a total of over 3,500,000,000 leaflet units, covering a range from single-unit leaflets to 48-page booklets, were set, printed and dispatched—the largest percentage of them being rushed through to meet delivery dates.

b. *Packaging and trucking* where the responsibility of the PWD Leaflet Section which maintained a special military unit consisting of one officer and eighty enlisted men with twenty-five trucks, for this purpose. In the case of one or two leaflets, in connection with which the time element was of paramount importance (for example, the daily newssheets), the finished job was packed into leaflet bombs at the printers and immediately rushed by the trucking unit to the desired airfields. In all other cases, the finished job was picked up from the printer, brought back to the packaging unit for packing into bombs and delivered to the various airfields as needed.

The Leaflet Section took delivery on 75,277 bombs, of which approximately 14,000 were still on hand on VE-Day, and another 6,000 were shipped to the Continent. The remaining 55,000 were packed with leaflets at the rate of approximately 4,000 bombs per month. The unit's trucks averaged some 18,230 miles per week on pick-up and delivery trips to the various printers and airfields.

In September 1944, the PWD Leaflet Section moved to Paris (leaving the Rear Section at Headquarters Eighth Air Force) and arranged for a comparatively small amount of printing for distribution by the Army groups to be done by local printers in Paris and Brussels, where local stocks of paper, as well as requisitions from HM Stationery Office, were used. When the Leaflet Section writing team was stationed in Paris, all tactical leaflet type-setting was done by commercial firms in Paris and reproduction proofs were forwarded to London and Brussels. However, since the majority of leaflets were dropped by British-based aircraft and United Kingdom printing facilities were superior to those available on the Continent, the great majority of the leaflets, and all of the publications, continued to be printed in the United Kingdom.

2. Army Groups

The problems in Army Group leaflet production varied widely. In the Twenty-first Army Group, lack of facilities at Army levels necessitated production of tactical leaflets at Group. In the Twelfth Army Group, the principal output was of the newspapers "Frontpost" and "Feldpost", with only about a dozen different general tactical leaflets produced in addition. No leaflets were produced by the Sixth Army Group, the production job being done at Army level in this case.

The Army Groups, because of their rear-area locations, were generally able to utilize local civilian printing plants for their production, giving them flexibility in layout, type faces and, when possible, use of colour. However, because of their distance from the Army teams, transportation provided a serious bottleneck, especially in the case of artillery leaflets produced at group for distribution by Armies. The failure to provide organic transportation for psychological warfare units was a serious handicap, both at Army Group and Armies.

A comparatively small number of higly skilled personnel was required for leaflet production: absolutely essential were one bi-lingual leaflet writer with previous writing experience, a skilled layout man and an officer to supervise printing operations. These, with the necessary enlisted men for clerical and printing jobs are the basic personnel for leaflet production at both Army Groups and Armies.

3. Army

The most difficult production job of all, that of turning out combat leaflets at short notice under field conditions, was performed by the Army psychological warfare teams. Those which concentrated especially on volume production of local tactical leaflets were the First, Third, Ninth and Seventh Army PW units. A considerable proportion of their production was done on mobile presses, but local facilities were utilized wherever possible because of the greater variety of format and larger volume possible.

In the matter of mobile production equipment, tremendous improvisation was required. Many printing trucks were equipped with Davidson presses capable of turning out only 4,000 leaflets per hour. The Webbendorfer press, which later became almost standard equipment, was able to print as many as 36,000 leaflets per hour but possessed the limitation of requiring special-sized paper. Often, only a small variety of type faces, some of them not ideal for leaflets, were available. Colour equipment, too, was usually lacking and during this campaign the value of colour in attracting attention to leaflets, especially when snow covered the front, was well established.

Transportation was again a tremendous problem, especially since the Army teams were required to print and pack leaflets in large volume for firing by artillery at lower echelons often long distances away over front-line roads. By the end of the campaign, most of these problems, and the equally serious one of training personnel for leaflet production, had been overcome to the extent that the Army teams were able to fullfill almost any leaflet production mission requested by lower echelons, or required by the tactical situation. An example of this was the production by the Seventh Army team of leaflets ready for firing against the town of Forbach within twelve hours from the time of the initial request being received.

5. DISTRIBUTION

Ideally, a leaflet operation should use all methods of distribution; the artillery for pinpoint local tactical leaflets, fighter bombers for tactical targets out of reach of artillery, medium bombers for close-in strategic and semi-tactical leaflets and heavy bombers for strategic leaflets aimed at enemy civilians far behind the line. In this campaign, however, due to the superior production facilities in the United Kingdom, and the fact that the only aircraft continuously under the operational control of PWD were the Special Leaflet Squadron of the Eight Air Force, the great bulk of SHAEF leaflets, both strategic and tactical, were distributed by United Kingdom-based heavy bombers. (See Exhibit 4.) The medium bombers were used for a few weeks after D-Day for special tactical leaflet missions, but as soon as they moved to the Continent, these operations ceased owing to lack of communications and transportation facilities. From then until the closing months of the war when arrangements were made for the distribution of the Twelfth Army Group weekly newspaper "Frontpost", little use was made of the medium bombers of the Ninth Air Force.

1. Air
   a. *Special Leaflet Squadron.* The most effective leaflet distribution by PWD-SHAEF was done by a squadron of heavy bombers especially assigned for leaflet operations by the Eighth Air Force. This Special Leaflet Squadron sent out an average of ten aircraft per night, weather permitting. These aircraft went out singly each covering as many as five targets per night selected by the Leaflet Section, PWD, SHAEF. This squadron accomplished the bulk of the leaflet distribution from the United Kingdom and was used primarily for the distribution of general tactical leaflets on targets on all sectors of the front, at the request of the Army Groups.

   The Leaflet Section, PWD, SHAEF, Rear, which was located at Headquarters Eighth Air Force, received by wire requests direct from the Army Groups and Armies for "Nachrichten" and standard general tactical leaflets, such as "Safe Conduct", "You Are Surrounded," etc., on targets in their areas. Based on these requests, the Leaflet Section made up each morning a list of targets and loads for the available planes for that night and telephoned them direct to the Operations Officer of the squadron.

   This was the only air force unit which was permanently and directly under the operational control of a psychological warfare organization, and it enabled PWD to deliver leaflets to any targets they selected at the time when they were most needed.

   The tremendous advantages of a special leaflet squadron are obvious. In addition to making it possible to direct leaflets to targets when they were most needed, it also made it possible for PWD to write and produce special leaflets with assurance that they would be able to get distribution of the leaflets in the areas for which they were intended. This enabled them to write messages addressed specifically to the inhabitants of a particular town or region, greatly increasing the effectiveness of the leaflets.

   In the closing days of the campaign when the demand for leaflets on the demoralized enemy was at its height, the Eighth Air Force made an additional squadron available for leaflet operations, but soon after this unit became available, VE-Day put an end to the leaflet operations.

   b. *Special Leaflet Missions*
      (1) Heavy bombers. At the request of PWD, the Eighth Air Force, on several occasions, made available heavy bombers for special leaflet missions. Regular bombing missions, however, obviously had priority, and it was only on a few special occasions, such as the attempt on Hitler's life on 20 July 1944, that the air forces were willing to make this special lift available.
      (2) Medium bombers. Medium bombers of the Ninth Air Force, based in the United Kingdom, were made available for special tactical leaflet missions for several weeks after D-Day, but when the Ninth Air Force moved to the Continent, the lack of communications and transportation facilities made it impossible to continue this operation. In the closing months of the war, these aircraft were also made available for special leaflet missions to distribute the Twelfth Army Group weekly newspaper "Frontpost".
      (3) Fighter bombers. The tactical air command supporting each Army made available fighter bombers for special leaflet missions to pinpoint local tactical targets. These missions were flown at the request of the Army PW liaison officer and made an extremely valuable contribution to the leaflet operation. Regular operational missions, however, had priority, and on some occasions, particularly during periods of great ground activity, the aircraft were not available for leaflet missions when most needed.

   c. *Regular Bombing Missions.*
      (1) Royal Air Force. The bombers of the Royal Air Force carried bundles of leaflets on their regular operational missions over enemy territory. These leaflets were released through the flare chute at or near the target and in this way, very substantial quantities of leaflets were distributed over enemy territory. The disadvantages of this system was that PID, which coordinated this operation, had no information before the mission of the target to be attacked and, therefore, had no control over the selection of leaflets or the quantities of leaflets which were dropped on each target. Also, leaflets dropped loose at bombing altitudes often drifted considerable distances before reaching the ground.
      (2) Eighth Air Force. On each bombing mission of the Eighth Air Force, a maximum of twelve aircraft were loaded with leaflet bombs. Each aircraft carried ten leaflet bombs so that on a mission, a maximum of 9,600,000 leaflet units could be distributed. Arrangements were made with the Eighth Air Force to give the Leaflet Section, PWD, SHAEF, Rear, which was located at the Headquarters, Eighth Air Force, the targets when the mission was planned, so that they were

able to specifiy the leaflets and the quantities which were to be dropped on each target. This had the obvious advantage of allowing PWD to specify a reasonable quantity, and the proper leaflet, for each target, and also, to avoid covering the same target with the same leaflet on successive missions. (See Exhibit 7.)

As the Royal Air Force and the Eighth Air Force usually went to targets deep in Germany which were beyond the range of the Special Leaflet Squadron, they were used primarily for the distribution of strategic leaflets addressed to the German civilian population.

2. Aircraft and Equipment.

a. *Heavy, medium and fighter bombers* were used for leaflet distribution during the Western European campaign. Each possessed certain unique qualifications for the particular task performed, and the use of all three types of aircraft was essential to the successful execution of the leaflet effort. In this campaign, however, due to the superior production facilities in the United Kingdom, and the fact that the Special Leaflet Squadron was the only distributing unit continuously under the operational control of PWD, the great bulk of SHAEF leaflets, both strategic and tactical, were distributed by that unit. This was not an ideal arrangement as much of this distribution could have been done more economically and with greater accuracy in daylight operations by medium and fighter bombers based on the Continent had these aircraft been made permanently available for special leaflet operations.

b. *Methods of Dropping.*

Originally, leaflet dropping by the USAAF was done by means of bundles fitted with an aneroid device designed to release the binding and free the leaflets at a given altitude. In practice, however, these aneroids did not function satisfactorily, and it became obvious that some more efficient method of distribution was needed. Obviously, a leaflet bomb, the trajectory of which would permit a reasonably accurate drop, and which would open to release leaflets at a low altitude was required. Two types of leaflet bombs, the T-1 and the T-3, were eventually accepted as standard for use in this theater by the USAAF.

(1) The T-1 bomb. All leaflets distributed by the Eighth Air Force, both on special missions and daylight bombing operations, were, after May 1944, carried in the T-1 leaflet bomb, a cylindrical, laminated, paper container, 60" long and 18" in diameter, fitted with a British 860A barometric nose fuse. This fuse functioned at approximately 2,000 feet, activating a primer cord which destroyed the container and released the leaflets. Use of this bomb simplified leaflet handling by units, and above all, avoided the extremely wide dispersion resulting from release at the altitudes of 20,000 feet and above at which B-17s and B-24s usually operated. Each bomb contained approximately 80,000 leaflet units, and tests indicated that under normal weather conditions, these would be scattered over an area of roughly one square mile. Ten of these bombs were carried by each aircraft on daylight operations and twelve in the adapted bomb bay of B-24s of the Special Squadron.

(2) T-3 bombs. Used exclusively by fighter bombers and on some missions by mediums, the T-3 leaflet bomb consisted of a converted M-26 metal flare case, 50" long and 8" in diameter, with a streamlined nose and tail fin to assist trajectory. This bomb could hold up to 15,000 leaflet units. As many as nine T-3 bombs were carried by fighter bombers and twenty by B-26s. Either an American M-111 clockwork fuze, or a British 860A barometric fuze was fitted.

c. *Types of Aircraft.*

(1) Heavy Bombers. Heavy bombers possessed the obvious advantages for leaflet operations of superior range and load-carrying capacity. As used in the Special Leaflet Squadron of the Eighth Air Force, each B-24 could drop 960,000 leaflet units on as many as five separate targets per sortie. In the operations of the Special Squadron, the large number of targets covered per mission and the efficiency of enemy air defenses necessitated night operations by aircraft flying singly. Although the leaflet bombing was done from high altitude at night by instruments, the wide dispersion of leaflets after the bombs burst gave sufficient coverage, and prisoner reaction figures show conclusively that a large percentage of leaflets dropped by the Special Squadron heavies reached their target area.

(2) Medium Bombers. Leaflet missions by Ninth Bomber Command B-26s were carried out in daylight at medium altitudes, with each aircraft dropping

20 T-3s or 6 T-1 leaflet bombs, or approximately 480,000 leaflet units. Daylight operations at lower altitudes permitted greater accuracy, but of course the range of mediums was considerably less than that of heavies, and the daylight missions necessitated formation flying and fighter escort, which reduced flexibility to some extent.

(3) Fighter Bombers. Pinpoint low-altitude leafleting of tactical targets beyond artillery range was the job of the fighter bombers of the various tactical air commands. P-47s were able to carry six T-3 bombs (three clustered under each wing) and sometimes nine (with three additional in the belly tank position) giving them a maximum load of 135,000 leaflet units. The accuracy of their low-level bombing, and the proximity of their bases to Army teams producing tactical combat leaflets made fighter bombers the ideal instrument for dissemination of these leaflets to areas immediately behind the front lines. Distribution by fighter bombers was carried out by means of special leaflet missions arranged through the air commands.

3. Artillery

Because of its accuracy, economy and availability, field artillery is the ideal instrument for the distribution of all tactical leaflets to targets within its range. The employment of artillery for leafleting can be traced back to the French use of the 75 mm. field piece for propaganda purposes on the Western Front in 1918. In this war, the idea was first put into practice with the British 25-pounder during the Tunisian campaign of 1942-1943.

Despite this previous battle use of artillery leaflets, this method of dissemination, although a known and accepted fact, was, because of lack of information on previous operations, still in the experimental stage when the Allied Armies landed in Normandy on D-Day, 1944. With the first psychological warfare unit (then constituted as a Mobile Radio Broadcasting Company) which landed soon after D-Day, came an artillery liaison officer. On D plus six, the first six rounds of artillery leaflets, mimeographed for a local situation, were fired, and proved their efficacy by netting six prisoners. By the end of June 1944, 900 rounds of propaganda shells had been fired on the First US Army sector alone. Artillery leafleting continued on an increasing scale on all of the Allied army sectors in the West until VE-Day, and proved itself to be one of the most effective weapons used by psychological warfare.

a. *Weapons*

The basic weapon used by American units for firing propaganda shells was the 105 mm. howitzer, M2 or M2 A1. This piece, with the shell and fuse commonly used, gave an average maximum range of 8,000 yards, enabling leaflets to reach as far back as battalion, regimental, and sometimes, division command posts. The shell used for leaflets was the 105 mm. smoke shell M84, HC, BE, W/PD, from which the smoke cannister was removed. This shell held approximately 500 artillery-size (4"×6¾") leaflets. An M54 fuse was used for ranges up to 8,000 yards, and the M67 fuse was used experimetally for utilization of the full range of the 105—up to 12,000 yards. This piece, shell and fuse were standard US weapons in almost universal use, and were most desirable from a psychological warfare viewpoint because of their availability and range, and the familiarity of artillery personnel with them.

Although experiments were made with the propaganda use of other artillery weapons, the 105 mm. in the US area, and the 25-pounder in the British were the mainstays of the artillery leafleting effort. Limited use was made of the 155 mm. smoke shell, which could hold up to 1,500 leaflets, and was capable of greater range. When firing is at ranges of over 5,000 yards, however, it is generally impossible to observe where shells burst except by aerial observation, which is often unavailable. This is somewhat of a drawback to the use of longer-range artillery weapons than the 105.

b. *Control*.

Control over artillery leaflet dissemination was the responsibility of the artillery liaison officer attached to Army psychological warfare units. In practice, the job of his section involved the performance of all necessary tasks from the time leaflets came off the press until they were fired by artillery units. Artillery liaison involved four principal duties:

(1) Liaison with Army ordnance and ammunition officers to insure a continuous flow of ammunition for propaganda purposes.
(2) Liaison with artillery sections at all echelons for arrangements for leaflet firing.

(3) Modification and loading of ammunition, and its delivery to depots, ASPs, division or field artillery batteries as required.

(4) Assistance to artillery units in firing of propaganda shells.

Experience proved, that because of their specialized nature, none of these tasks could be successfully relegated to other units.

Requests for artillery leaflet "shoots" were generally passed by division or corps personnel (often the G-2) through psychological warfare personnel operating at that level either as liaison officers or in amplifier units, to the artillery liaison section of the Army psychological warfare unit, which would then coordinate all details of the operation. Usually, the loaded leaflet shells would be delivered to the S-4 or ordnance officer of the unit performing the firing. The S-3 or operations officer would then allot shells to the various batteries, basing his distribution on the best information on local enemy dispositions available from the unit S-2 or intelligence officer.

c. *Advantages of Artillery Leafleting*

The distribution of leaflets by artillery possessed several distinct advantages over other methods:

(1) Accuracy. In local tactical situations artillery leaflets could ordinarily be placed within a few hundred yards, at least, of enemy positions within range. Although greater saturation could be obtained by means of air drops, it was the estimate of one PW officer that up to five times as many air-dropped as artillery leaflets were required to insure pinpoint coverage of a given position.

(2) Availability. Along any active ground front there will be artillery positions, and the fact that psychological warfare units at lower echelons are attached to ground rather than air units makes the coordination and arrangement of artillery leafleting simpler than air drops. Also, in the case of air leaflet missions, such operations must be scheduled and special units detailed for the performance of the task. With artillery leaflets, the only requirement is the delivery of filled shells to the appropriate unit and coordination with that unit's commander. Finally, and extremely important in a theater such as Western Europe, is the fact that artillery is not affected by adverse weather conditions. During this campaign many air missions scheduled for coordination with important tactical operations had to be cancelled or postponed because aircraft could not get off the ground.

(3) Economy. The firing of propaganda shells requires no extra risk of men and equipment and little extra employment of service personnel, in contrast to air missions.

d. The obvious disadvantages of artillery leafleting are lack of range and lack of flexibility. The latter factor is especially important during fluid situations when artillery units are frequently on the move and, therefore, unavailable. During periods of breakthrough and pursuit, artilery can seldom be utilized to full-advantage for leaflet operations, but in relatively static situations it is, within its range, the ideal method of tactical leaflet dissemination.

4. Other methods

a. *Balloons.*

Small quantities of leaflets, mostly "black", were regularly disseminated by British agencies operating first in the United Kingdom and later on the Continent, using balloons especially adapted for this work, designed to release bundles of leaflets at a given time after the balloons had been set free.

b. *Patrols.*

Additional small numbers of leaflets, often of a local tactical nature, were frequently scattered behind the enemy's lines on various sectors by scouting patrols and agents at night. This means of augmenting leaflet distribution is especially valuable because leaflets are almost certain of reaching the hands of enemy troops. However, the leaflets created an added risk that the passage of a patrol or agent would be given away.

6. RESULTS

1. Psychological warfare deals with such intangibles as the comparative influence of various factors on the thought processes of the enemy. It is, therefore, impossible to measure the results in exact mathematical terms. However, a mass of material dealing with enemy counter-measures, prisoner of war reactions, as disclosed in polls and interviews, and official reports by Allied ground units, gives convincing evidence of the effectiveness of the leaflet operation in Western Europe. (See Exhibit 6.)

2. The following examples selected from this mass of evidence divide into two categories: (1) indirect reactions—penalties, warnings and other examples of counter action; and (2) direct reactions—statements by individuals, results of official surveys and evidence reported by our ground forces.

a. *Indirect Reactions*

(1) "Goebbels gives warning—'Very clever leaflets. Through his mouthpiece, Karl Siegbold, Gobbels last night broadcast a warning to Germans against Allied leaflets. German soldiers and civilians were told, 'There is not a single sentence in these leaflets which does not want to do us harm. They are addressed to the weak points which exist in every nation. It ought to be below our dignity to read what the leaflets say. They are weapons, and we must be careful with all weapons.

There are two kinds of leaflets. The first is a small size newssheet, very cleverly done, with impressive maps and pictures. It has a completely bona fide appearance. But among correct and truthful reports it contains innumerable half-truths, omissions, exaggerations. Indeed, every news item, every short article, every comment contains a small—only just noticeable—amount of distrust in the actions of the German High Command.

The second type of leaflet is different. It is openly treacherous, grinning with lies and broad impudence, etc. etc.'" London Daily Express, 30 Sept. 1944.

(2) "Captured German soldiers say that nobody below the rank of major is allowed to pick up leaflets dropped on them by the Allies. An army order told them: 'These leaflets invite you to desert; if you do, you will be taken to England and run the risk of death by V-1. After that, you will be shipped to the United States or Canada for life-long hard labor, or exchanged for an American or British paratroop—of whom we have captured thousands—tried by court martial, and shot.'" London Daily Mail, 13 August 1944.

(3) Penalties ordered by German civil courts for reading and distributing Allied leaflets:—

August 1944—Aachen—2-months imprisonment
September 1944—Hamburg—2-years imprisonment.
October 1944—Innsbruck—death sentence.

(4) „In the early hours of November 10th, the enemy dropped leaflets 'Nachrichten für die Truppe' dated November 9th. They bring, in partly very clever, partly somewhat clumsy form, the news of yesterday. Even the most self-respecting soldier is tempted to read these news-sheets, since our own Frontkurier usually does not arrive until the late afternoon—or even three to four days later. There must be some way for us to bring the news to our men earlier than the enemy in order to kill the solidiers' curiosity." Communication from German front line CO to higher headquarters.

(5) "At this point the enemy leaflet comes out with a notorious objective article. Whoever yields to the temptation reads the article, in spite of all prohibitions, will be puzzled at first. Here is a cool, objective, German military style. Not a word too many or too few. The article contains an account of the course of the battle during the last few days which exactly corresponds to the facts. The reader is amazed to find that this dicussion contains no lies. What he does not notice, of course, is the fact that this is the exact moment when the devil is on the spot leading him into temptation. For now comes the concluding part of the report which apparently was so objective. Again in the same cool, matter-of-fact style, it is stated that certain persons are responsible for the outcome of the battle—an SS general is named here, an army general there. In the end, the soldier is asked when he will finally give up this senseless struggle. We wish to make the following remarks in this connection: 1. The enemy is using this type of propaganda more frequently; it is assumed that there will be more of it and we must, therefore, be on our guard. 2. On the whole, it can be assumed that the order to destroy enemy leaflets or hand them in is carried out well. 3. In spite of this, however, this order must be stressed again and again every time the troops go into action." Wehrmacht High Command Bulletin for the Officers' Corps.

(6) "The enemy on his part is employing all means in order to shatter the steadfastness of the German people on which everything depends. He seeks especially by means of clever propaganda to disintegrate the German Forces and to paralyze their will to resist. He will not succeed in this. However, it would be wrong to think that such attempts are so futile that they

need not be taken seriously ... (signed) Blaskowitz." Order from Commander-in-Chief, Army Group G.

b. *Direct Reactions*
   (1) "Seventy-seven percent of the prisoners taken had read our leaflets." Anthony Eden, House of Commons, July 1944.
   (2) Estimated percentages of prisoners who had seen and who had been influenced by leaflets (based on polls of sample groups of prisoners of war):—

Date	Combat Area	Percent who saw leaflets	Percent influenced (of those who saw leaflets)
1944:			
26/6—28/6	Cherbourg	77	
1/7—17/7	Carentan—St. Lo	69	
26/7—27/7	St. Lo	84	76
1/8—10/8	St. Malo—Le Mans	24	37
September	Western Front	30	45
15/10—19/10	Aachen	64	37
November	1st US Army	80	
15/19—31/12	1, 3, 9th US Army	66	78
1945:			
1/1—31/1	"	69	75
1/2—28/2	"	87	72
1/3—15/3	"	90	79

PWD/SHAEF Intelligence Section report

   (3) Estimated percentages of civilians in medium-sized towns in central Germany reached by Allied leafleting (based on polls of the populations of Hersfeld, Marburg and Eschwege):—

Percent read leaflets	Percent of those who had seen leaflets and who read		
	Newsseets	Eisenhower Proclamation	Other leaflets
30	32	23	57

PWD/SHAEF Intelligence Section report

These figures are a particularly impressive indication of the penetration of strategic leafleting to the German civilian population because none of the towns polled had been leafleted by the Eighth Air Force, the Royal Air Force or the Special Squadron.

   (4) "It is impossible to determine the exact effectiveness of air drops, but it is a fact that over 80% of all prisoners we have netted on the Brest Peninsula have come in with leaflets in their possession ..... Korvettenkapitän Fritz Otto, now a prisoner, informed us that with leaflets falling all around his troops he found himself leading a 'bunch of neurotics' and gave the whole thing up, coming over to us." Twelfth Army Group Report.
   (5) "When the final count came in for Le Havre, it showed 11,302 prisoners out of 12,000 garrison. Analysis shows that over 75% had leaflets on them." Twenty-first Army Group Report.
   (6) "Out of a sample group of 200 prisoners captured in and around Aachen in the middle of October, approximately 50% had leaflets on their person at the time of their capture." PWD-SHAEF Intelligence Section Report.
   (7) "P/Ws reported that the PWB leaflet containing the test of Aachen ultimatum had influenced them to desert. One, a Prussophobe Bavarian, decided to desert after reading this leaflet, took a Viennese comrade along, persuaded 11 others to join, marched to the US lines waving the leaflets and white flags, and finally broadcast appeals over our public address system to remaining comrades." Twelfth Army Group Report.
   (8) "Despite strict orders not to read our leaflets, they are passed on and discussed constantly." Seventh US Army Report.
   (9) "Lt. Wisser, an ardent Nazi, declined to speak during the interrogation but later stated that 'unhappily, these leaflets have a great influence on the men and

constitute a serious threat to their morale' . . . . . The morale of the troops fighting against this army is seriously shaken. The enemy know that it is futile to fight tanks with guns, but they are afraid to surrender because they have been briefed on bad treatment. They believe they will be shot by 'de Gaulle troops'. These leaflets give them confidence. They have only one wish — to surrender. The obvious conclusion is to increase, if possible, the distribution of leaflets." Fifth Armored Division (First French Army) Report.

(10) "Prisoners taken during the operation against the Ardennes salient all claimed to have been deeply impressed by the leaflets. Even towards the end of the operation many German soldiers believed, until they found copies of our leaflets, that they were defending a flank under difficult circumstances but that the spearhead of the German attack had passed onto Liège, Brussels, and even Paris. When they learned the true state of affairs they were often ready to capitulate. Although no official figures are available, it would seem reasonable to estimate that more than half of the prisoners taken in the last week of December and during the month of January had seen our leaflets. A great many still had leaflets with them, and in most cases the leaflets proved to be those which had been dropped by high-level bombers in the interior of the salient." Third US Army Report.

7. CONCLUSIONS

Inasmuch as the detailed organization of any future psychological warfare leaflet operation must, of necessity, be governed by the nature and location of the campaign, the only conclusions presented in this report are certain broad, general aspects which the experience in the Western European Theater indicate should be basic to any future psychological warfare operation.

1. *Military Organization.* In order to obtain the close coordination with plans and operations necessary to make psychological warfare an effective part of a military operation, it is essential to have the organization responsible an integral part of the military organization. The security which is required in planning future operations makes it undesirable to disclose these plans to outside organizations, and without this advance information, it is impossible to intelligently plan a psychological warfare campaign to tie in with the military operation. Also, in liaison and coordination with lower echelons, it is much easier for a military representative of the commanding general to get results that a civilian representing some outside organization. The restrictions imposed on civilians in combat zones make it very difficult for them to operate and it is believed absolutely essential to have the psychological warfare organization basically military and directly responsible to military authority with a minimum of civilian specialists attached.

2. *Operational Control of Aircraft.* To produce maximum results, it is obviously essential for leaflet messages to be delivered to the desired target at a particular time. To accomplish this, it is necessary for the psychological warfare unit to have aircraft at its disposal which it can send to selected targets when required, and experience has shown that the only way that this can be done is to have certain aircraft assigned permanently and exclusively to leaflet operations. Although the Air Forces have been extremely cooperative, arrangements made with them at some echelons whereby they agreed to schedule special leaflet missions on request from the psychological warfare unit have not worked out satisfactorily. On this basis, it was obvious that regular combat missions had priority and quite naturally, very often during periods of great ground activity when leaflets were most needed, the aircraft were not available. It is, therefore, believed to be a basic and fundamental requirement that at all echelons of psychological warfare in future operations a sufficient number of aircraft be assigned permanently and exclusively to leaflet missions.

3. *Intelligence.* The results of leaflet operations cannot be assessed by means of photographs or examination of damaged installations. They are so intangible as to require the constant efforts of specialized personnel at all levels to determine, by means of surveillance of every conceivable source of information, the efficacy of given leaflets and of the over-all psychological warfare campaign. Above all, effective liaison must be maintained from the lowest to the highest level for the immediate transmission of all relevant intelligence of the effectiveness of propaganda and on the enemy situation and morale. The prompt receipt of this information is essential to the preparation of effective leaflets for future distribution.

APPENDIX "I"

PWD Organization Chart

PWD-SHAEF
21 APRIL 1944

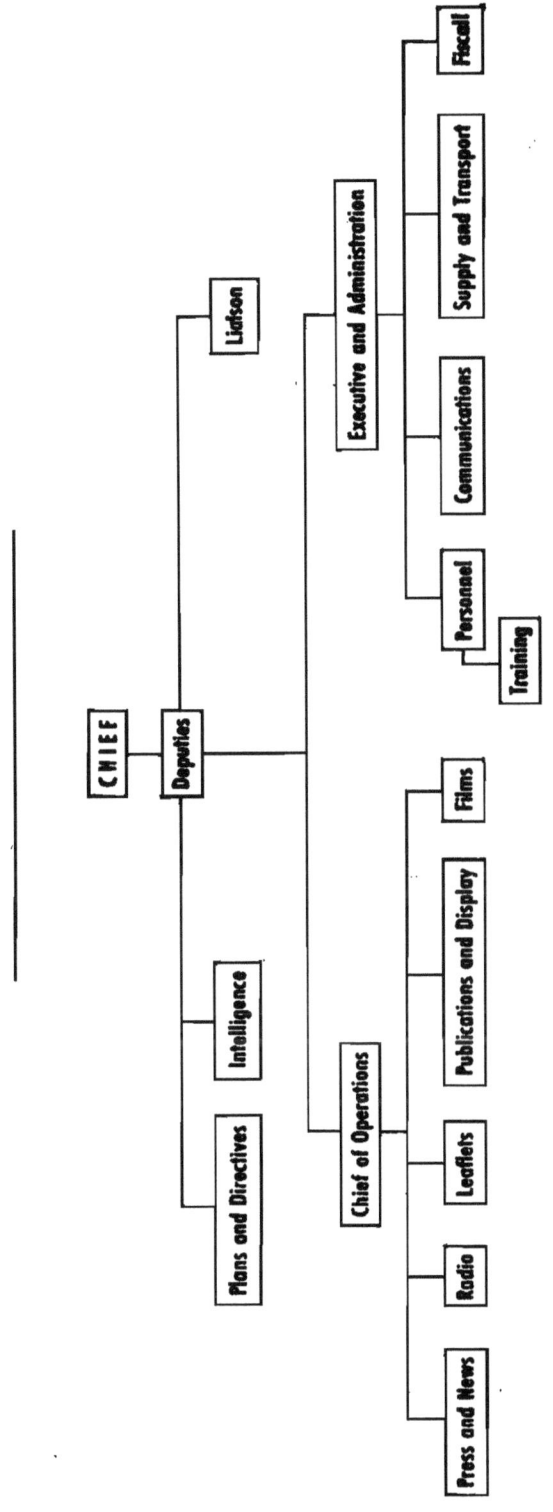

APPENDIX "J"

Organization Chart of Information Control Division, United States Forces, European Theatre, and Information Control Service, U.S. Group Control Council

(The pattern of organization shown in this chart was not achieved under PWD-SHAEF. However, it is included here since it was toward this kind of organization that PWD-SHAEF was aiming during the final weeks of its existence.)

Exhibit 1

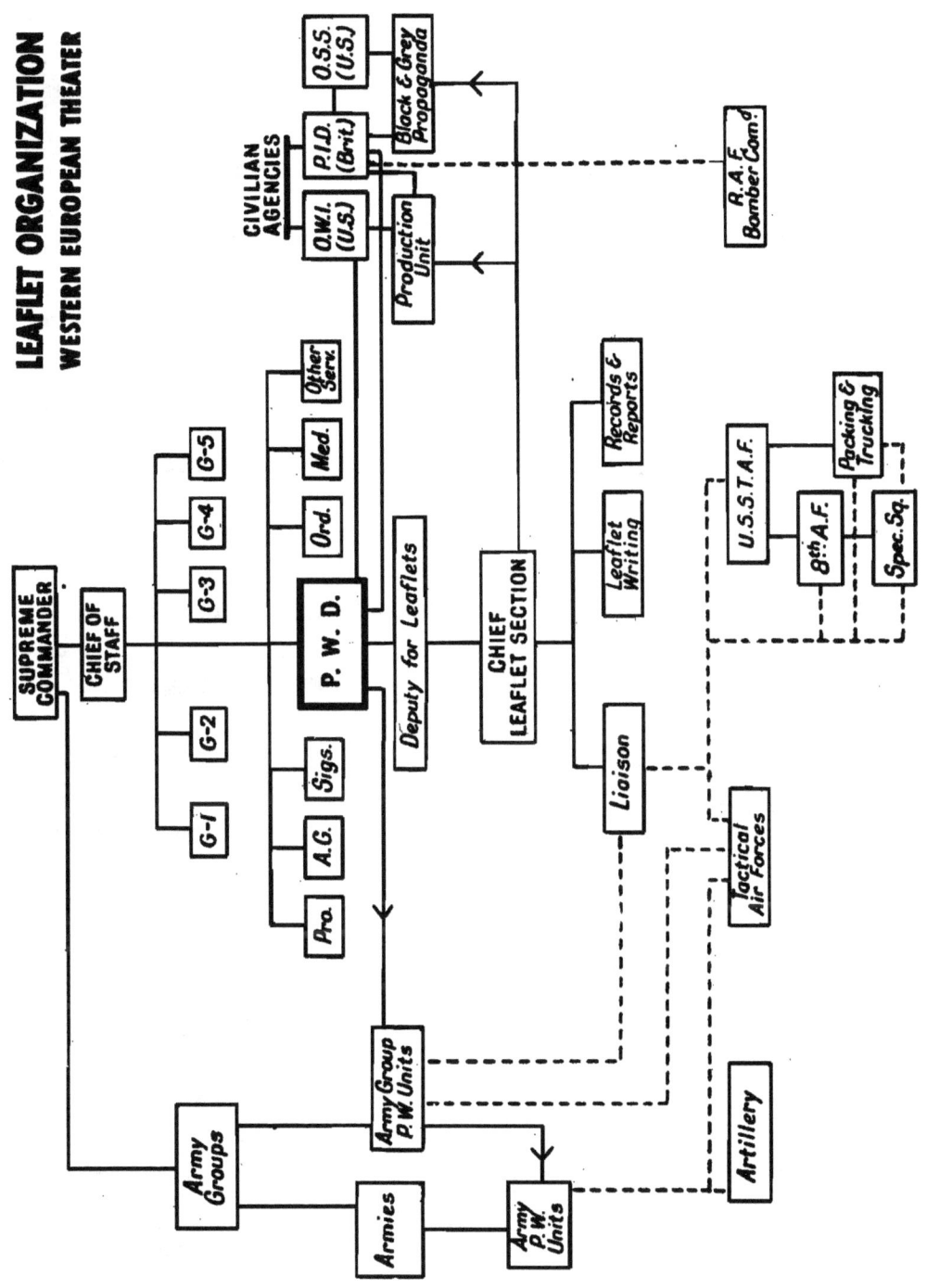

Exhibit 2

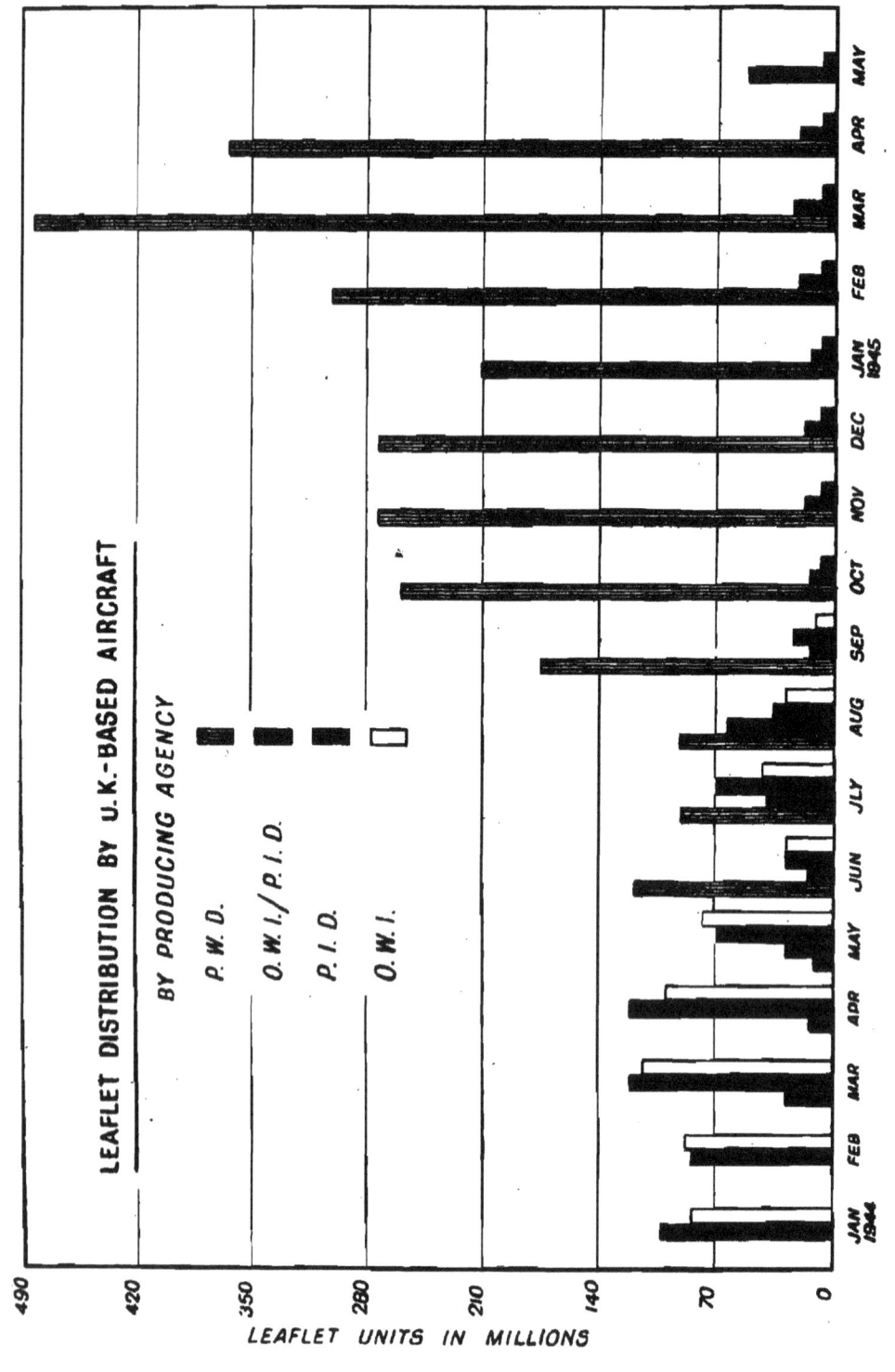

Exhibit 3

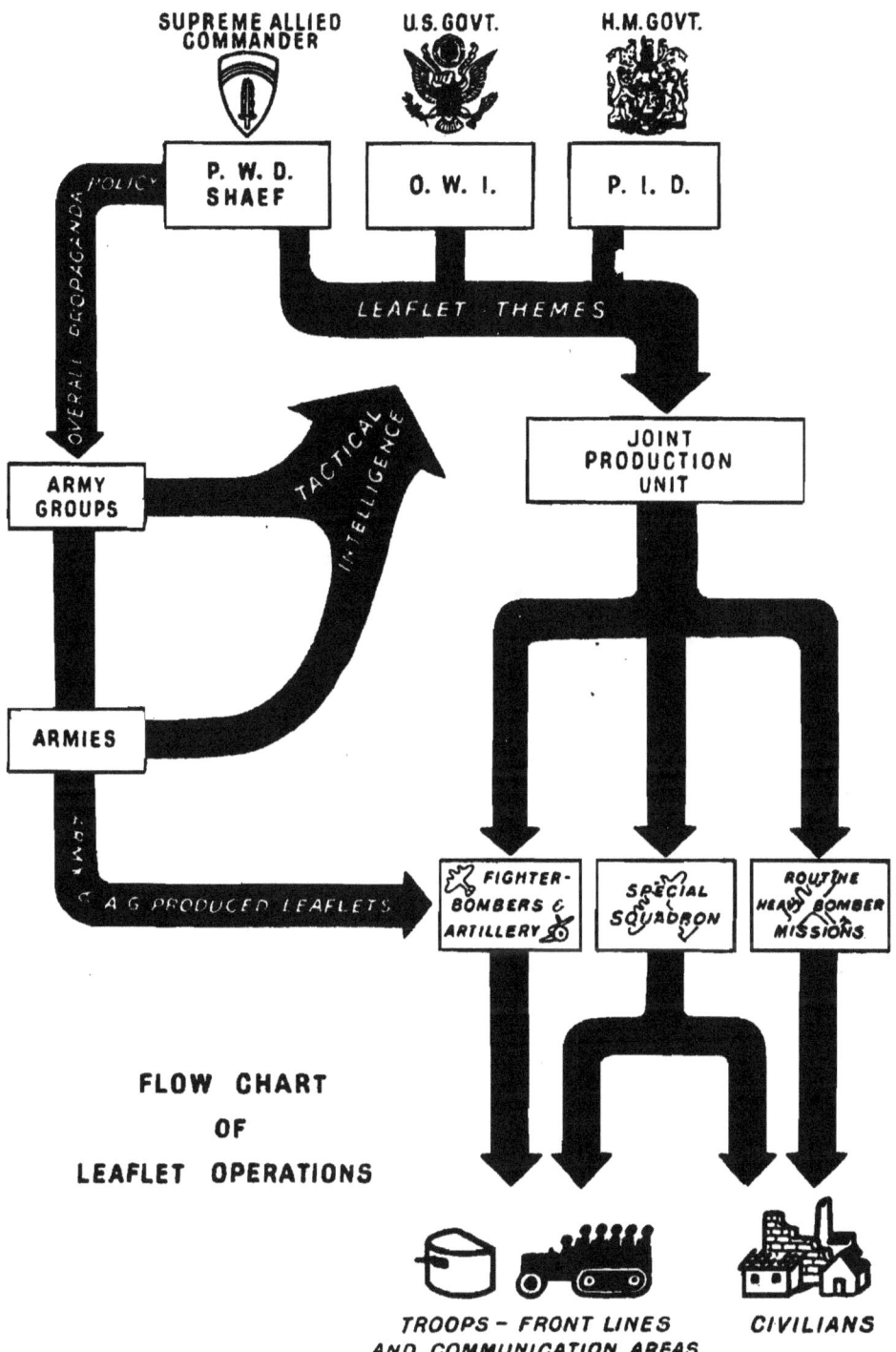

FLOW CHART OF LEAFLET OPERATIONS

131

The following pages bear samples of PWD/SHAEF leaflets. In each case, the German version is at the right, and the English translation of the text at the left.

Exhibit 9

ZG. 61 / The Safe Conduct was the most successful of all of the leaflets developed during the campaign. It is based on an idea first found in Russian combat leaflets, but its presentation as an elaborate, authoritative signed document is the result of work done by the PWD/SHAEF Leaflet Section. It was dropped in extremely large quantities, both as an individual drop and in drops mixed with other leaflets, throughout the campaign, and in prisoner surveys invariably rated far above all other leaflets.

TRANSLATION OF ZG 108

ONE MINUTE

which may save your life

Read the following six points carefully and thoroughly. They may mean for you the difference between life and death.

1. In a battle of material, valour alone cannot offset the inferiority in tanks, planes and artillery.

2. With the breaching of the Atlantic Wall and of the Eastern Front, the decision has fallen; Germany has lost the war.

3. You are not facing barbarians who delight in killing, but soldiers who would spare your life if possible.

4. But we can only spare those who do not force us, by senseless resistance, to use our weapons against them.

5. It is up to you to show us your intention by raising your arms, waving a handkerchief, etc., in an unmistakable manner.

6. Prisoners-of-war are treated decently, in a fair manner, as becomes soldiers who have fought bravely.

You must decide for yourself. But, in the event that you should find yourself in a desperate situation, remember what you have read.

EINE MINUTE

die Dir das Leben retten kann.

Lies die folgenden 6 Punkte gründlich und aufmerksam! Sie können für Dich den Unterschied zwischen Tod und Leben bedeuten.

1. Tapferkeit allein kann in diesen Materialschlachten den Mangel an Panzern, Flugzeugen und Artillerie nicht wettmachen.

2. Mit dem Fehlschlag im Westen und dem Zusammenbruch im Osten ist die Entscheidung gefallen: Deutschland hat den Krieg verloren.

3. Du stehst keinen Barbaren gegenüber, die am Töten etwa Vergnügen finden, sondern Soldaten, die Dein Leben schonen wollen.

4. Wir können aber nur diejenigen schonen, die uns nicht durch nutzlosen Widerstand zwingen, unsere Waffen gegen sie einzusetzen.

5. Es liegt an Dir, uns durch Hochheben der Hände, Schwenken eines Taschentuchs usw. deutlich Deine Absicht zu verstehen zu geben.

6. Kriegsgefangene werden fair und anständig behandelt, ohne Schikane - wie es Soldaten gebührt, die tapfer gekämpft haben.

Die Entscheidung musst Du selber treffen. Sollst Du aber in eine verzweifelte Lage geraten, so erwäge, was Du gelesen hast.

ZG. 108 / One of the most successful of the general tactical leaflets. It was designed for distribution to areas of stiff enemy resistance and again and again proved its effectiveness in prisoner returns. Its lack of any political appeal, and its short-term soldier-to-soldier language seems to have been among the factors of its success.

TRANSLATION OF Z.G. 86

You are now cut off!

In order to avoid needless bloodshed, this leaflet is being delivered to you.

You are now cut off. Allied units are already far in your rear. You have fought bravely, but from now on it would be senseless to continue fighting. You must give up or die — shortly before the end of the war.

You realize your situation. Now you must act accordingly. Every one of you must decide for himself. There is no time to be lost.

The Allies want to spare your lives and guarantee you decent treatment. But you must clearly indicate that you are quitting the fight.

ACT IMMEDIATELY!

Ihr seid jetzt abgeschnitten!

Um nutzloses Blutvergiessen zu ersparen, wird Euch dieses Flugblatt zugestellt.

Ihr seid jetzt abgeschnitten. Alliierte Einheiten stehen bereits weit hinter Euch. Ihr habt tapfer gekämpft, aber von jetzt an ist ein Weiterkämpfen nutzlos. Ihr müsst Euch ergeben oder knapp vor Kriegsende sterben.

> Ihr erkennt die Lage. Es gilt jetzt, dementsprechend zu handeln. Jeder muss für sich selbst entscheiden. Es ist keine Zeit zu verlieren.
>
> Die Alliierten wollen Euer Leben schonen und sichern Euch anständige Behandlung zu. Ihr müsst aber klar zu verstehen geben, dass Ihr aus dem Kampf scheidet.

HANDELT SOFORT!

ZG. 87 / A tactical "contingency" leaflet written to cover a commonly recurring situation and held ready for immediate drop whenever such a situation occurred.

ADVICE ON HOW
TO SAVE YOUR LIFE

Anybody who is in danger of being called up as a member of the Volkssturm should read the following advice very carefully. To follow these instructions carefully may make the difference between life and death.

1. If it is at all possible, avoid being called up by not registering, changing your address, or going underground among friends and sympathizers.

2. If you are called up and can't avoid it, obey the call-up.

3. Do not resist when they drive you into action. Seek cover in the best protected place you can find and wait.

4. Then, when the Allies attack, put your hands above your head and surrender. You will have done no harm to the Allies. They will do nothing to you.

Only those who follow this advice in every detail will survive in the great battle of material in the West. Volkssturm captured in action will be treated strictly according to the Geneva Convention and the rules of war and will be returned to their homes at the end of hostilities.

DEUTSCHER VOLKSSTURM
WEHRMACHT

ANWEISUNGEN ZUR LEBENSRETTUNG

Wer Gefahr läuft, vom Volkssturm erfasst zu werden, der lese die nachfolgenden Anweisungen genauestens. Ihre genaue Befolgung kann den Unterschied zwischen Tod und Leben bedeuten:

> Wenn irgend möglich, so entziehe Dich der Einberufung durch Nichtmelden, Wohnungswechsel oder « Untertauchen » unter Freunden und Gleichgesinnten.
>
> Kannst Du Dich der Einberufung nicht entziehen, so stelle Dich ordnungsgemäss.
>
> Leiste keinen Widerstand dagegen, wenn man Dich in den Einsatz treibt. Suche Deckung in einer möglichst geschützten Stelle und warte.
>
> Wenn dann die Alliierten angreifen, ergib Dich, indem Du die Hände hochhebst. Die Alliierten tun Dir nichts, Du hast ihnen auch nichts getan.

Nur wer diese Anweisungen genauestens befolgt, kommt in den Materialschlachten des Westens mit dem Leben davon. Kriegsgefangene des Volkssturms werden nach den Kriegsregeln und Bestimmungen der Genfer Konvention behandelt und kehren nach Kriegsende wieder nach Hause zurück.

WG 27 K

WG. 27 / A strategic leaflet which attacks the myth of a "Nation in Arms", corrodes the fabric of the Volkssturm plan and enlists the aid of German civilians in fighting the Nazi plan for raising an effective militia.

www.ingramcontent.com/pod-product-compliance
Lightning Source LLC
Chambersburg PA
CBHW050502110426
42742CB00018B/3336